WORRIER
TO
WARRIOR

---

7 STEPS TO UNCOVER
THE WARRIOR WITHIN AND
LIVE INCREDIBLY FULL EVERYDAY!

MARTIN SALAMA

© 2023 by
MARTIN SALAMA

All rights reserved. No part of this book may be reproduced in any form without permission in writing from the publisher, except in the case of brief quotations embodied in critical articles or reviews.

Martin Salama
Brooklyn, NY, USA
TheWarriorsLIFECode.com
ConnectwithMartin.com

First Edition

Written by Martin Salama
Edited by Heather Marie Harden
Cover and interior design: Heather Marie Harden

Library of Congress Cataloging-in-Publication Data
Salama, Martin. Worrier to Warrior: 7 Steps to UNCOVER the Warrior Within and Live Incredibly Full Everyday.
ISBN 979-8-9870061-1-5

We hope you enjoy this book from The Warrior's L.I.F.E. Code. Our goal is to provide encouraging and practical guides to standing up again after adversity and standing in your power. Blessings to you.

June 2023
Published by The Warrior's L.I.F.E. Code
Printed in the United States of America

Praise for
Worrier to Warrior

After reading Worrier to Warrior, I think you'll agree with me that Martin is like a breath of fresh, honest air, a man of extreme integrity who seeks the truth in all things. The book is ultimately a testament to the resilience of the human spirit and the immeasurably transformative power of taking life into one's own hands.

Genevieve Davis
Bestselling author of Magic Words and How to Use Them

I've always said that if someone wrote a book that took their whole life to learn the knowledge in, why not read it?

After reading and applying the information in Worrier to Warrior, you may discover your potential as you have never seen it before. Martin Salama delivers like no other.

Dr. Obom Bowen
Founder Underdog Millionaire ™ and the Millionaire Club

Martin has a message to share that you need to hear!

Barbara La Pointe
Host of Healing Broken Families podcast

Martin has the power to get people out of that place of being afraid of the crazy things life throws at us to a place where they appreciate life, are ready to take on the world, and are grateful for every opportunity they find throughout the day.

Ely Delaney
*Automated Systems Strategist and
Founder of Purple Knight Marketing*

Martin helps people shift their mindset through compelling storytelling and simple but effective methods.

Crystal Anne Compton
Host of the Life Magnetics podcast

Martin's fun and the way he explains things are easy to understand. Martin has the ability to explain very complex topics in a straightforward way. You can tell he's living what he's preaching.

Ani Rich
Host of the Intuitively Rich podcast

Martin Salama is a wealth of knowledge and an inspiration for all of us.

Sifu Rafael Gomez
Host of the Coaching Call podcast

Martin Salama is a great individual...for a "human" and "personal" conversation about life!

Ken Hannaman
Host of the Ungraduated Living podcast

Good energy, good message, great stories.

RJ Campbell
Co-Host of The Balanced Business Dad podcast

Martin has so much wisdom *and* he's fun to talk to.

Julie Hilsen
Host of the Love of Life Podcast

Martin brings great energy, enthusiasm, and fun...and offers great information.

Bob Brumm
Host of the Encouragement Engineering Podcast

Dedications

To my father, Ceasar Salama, Baruch Dayan HaEmet, who was the embodiment of "Don't take anything personally," a lesson that took me a long time to learn. His kindness and respect for everyone he met will never be forgotten. We miss you.

To my mother, Esther Salama, who rose from the tragedy of losing a child with grace and love to a position to help and support others who befall the same kind of tragedy. And who has built a strong loving family that will endure for generations.

To my brother Michael, Baruch Dayan HaEmet - You were in my life for a short time. For a very long time, your passing affected me in the wrong way. After many years, I was able to find my path and I know you are watching over me. Your short life has impacted so many people and will continue to for many years to come. My legacy is your legacy.

To my sisters and their husbands and children, thank you for your love and support. You all practice the values taught by Mom and Dad, especially "Unconditional Kindness". I love seeing your children carry on the community values instilled in us by our parents and grandparents. I know they will continue to be sources of light in our lives and the lives of their children and grandchildren.

To my children, Esther, Ceasar, Moe, and Claire - my love for you knows no bounds. Your return love is something I cherish dearly. As I watch you all grow into beautiful men and women, I feel such happiness knowing your values are well aligned with who you are.

To my son-in-law Jack and daughter-in-law Chloe, God has given Esther and Ceasar exactly the people they needed in their lives, thank you, I love you.

To my grandchildren, you have shown me the true meaning of unconditional love. Papa will always be there for you. May you be a great source of joy, happiness, and light for the world to appreciate and love.

To my stepchildren Moses, Sonya, and Ralph Bakst for accepting me into your lives with no expectations. For always keeping me on my toes. You all have such intelligence that I know will be an asset to all the people you come into contact with. If I have had an even minimal part in that, I am beyond happy.

To my new in-laws, Cookie and Ralph Setton, and my sisters and brothers-in-law, for accepting me into your family with open arms and have treated me as I have always been part of your lives.

To Sarita, words cannot express how much I love and appreciate you. You are my compass. You "get" me while also keeping me going in the right direction when my ADHD can take me all over the place. The words of the song "Better Place" are never too far away from me and it's because of you. I'm looking forward to so many more L.I.F.E. adventures together all over the world.

Acknowledgments

With Profound Gratitude to…

Almighty God - Who I call Hashem. When I came to understand the true meaning of "Surrender to God" is when everything began to click into place. I have always had a deep belief in HaShem, yet until I accepted that I can't do anything alone, without surrendering it to God, I usually found I was doubting myself. That was because I needed Hashem's guidance. Recently I learned the Hebrew word Bitachon, meaning reliance on Hashem. It is with Bitachon that I accomplished this book.

Heather Harden — I definitely believe the day we met was exactly a Cycle of A's moment. The past two-plus-year journey started when I listened to my gut and told myself, this is what I need right now if I want to get my message out there. You have steered me in the right direction while completely understanding my message. You have helped me build my Warrior's L.I.F.E. Code message in a manner that keeps me within my values while also staying authentic with no compromise along the way.

Josh Harden — You came onto the team along with Heather, and right away I appreciated your commitment, talent, authenticity, and willingness to be vulnerable. When you asked me to coach you, I was honored and excited at the same time. You gave me the opportunity to have proof of concept. You would show up every time to our coaching calls, just willing to learn and change. I've said it before, I am so proud of the man you have become. You are my poster boy.

Genevieve Davis — Your coaching, mentoring, and guidance came into my L.I.F.E. at the perfect time. I had been reading your books for a few years before I had the opportunity to be personally coached by you. You connected the dots that were right in front of me but I couldn't see how to connect them. Since then I am honored to call you a friend and humbled that you were willing to write my foreword. Please never stop teaching Magic. The world needs it and more importantly, the world needs you.

Dr. Obom — Your belief in me at the very beginning of our relationship gave me the confidence I needed to create the program I knew I had within me. Your teachings have helped me understand I am my own limitations, and as such I have no limitations. You honored my religious commitments when others merely accepted them. I hope to always be your "Favorite Jew" LOL.

Ana & Miracle Bowen — For showing me that when you show the world exactly who you are, with no airs or apologies, the world will see you exactly as you are - authentic and beautiful.

Afiya Al-Fayiz — The technical and accountability side of UMBA - For holding my space exactly where I needed it and showing me how to grow my message by holding my hand as well as pushing me out of my comfort zone.

Kimberly Crowe and Gini Trask — For giving me the space to grow and learn on stages with Oreo feedback when it was called for.

Forbes Riley — For giving me that kick in the pants I needed, while showing your love and caring at the same time. You have a gift, keep sharing it with the world.

Donna Kozik — Your friendship and guidance over the past 10 years have been invaluable. Thank you for being a good friend.

Kelly Sabbagh — For calling me right after my divorce and informing me that you were my matchmaker. Then holding my hand through the process of going back into the world of dating. The day you called to tell me about Sarita and insisted I take her out was a defining moment in my life. Thank you for bringing the love of my life to my world.

Bruce D. Schneider and all of the people at iPEC (Institute for Professional Excellence in Coaching) — For teaching me, if you stretch your mind, you can always change yourself for the better, and by understanding your "Core Energy" you can raise your own energy level. Especially at a time when I really needed to understand how my energy was affecting my life.

Arthur Brown — For your youthful exuberance. Keep spreading your message and your magic.

Odia Kalala — For bringing my tech understanding into the 21st century, and for your excitement when you share something or learn something new.

The Rabbis — Who have guided me along my spiritual journey, including but not limited to: Rabbi Moshe Shamah, Rabbi Sam Kassin, Rabbi Steven Amon, and Rabbi Ezra Labaton Baruch Dayan HaEmet.

To all the others like Laurie Masters, Ely Delaney, Susan Kerby, Angel Tuccy, Patsy Sanders, Catharine O'Leary, JD Wildflower, Frank King, and Jimmy the Doorman who helped solidify the concept of this book in the physical world, thank you for showing up in my L.I.F.E. at times that made sense. You've proven to me there is no such thing as coincidences. Everything happens for a reason.

"Change begins at the end of your comfort zone."

Roy T. Bennett

Contents

Dedications	5
Acknowledgments	7
Contents	11
Foreword	13
Introduction	17
PART 1: TOOLS FOR SUCCESS	**23**
Chapter 1 — Admission, Cleansing & Celebration	25
Chapter 2 — Origins of The Warrior's L.I.F.E. Code	31
Chapter 3 — Success Stories	35
Chapter 4 — The Cycle of A's (Ask, Act, Attitude)	41
PART 2: DEEP DIVE INTO TRANSFORMATION	**49**
Chapter 5 — Stop	51
Chapter 6 — Think	59
Chapter 7 — Respond	65
Chapter 8 — Putting It All Together	69
Chapter 9 — Words of Encouragement	75
PART 3: REFLECTION FOR CHANGE	**77**

Chapter 10 — Reflection Sequence Overview	79
Chapter 11 — Unlock	83
Chapter 12 — Unleash	93
Chapter 13 — Navigate	99
Chapter 14 — Choose	111
PART 4: ACTION FOR CHANGE	**119**
Chapter 15 — Action Sequence Overview	121
Chapter 16 — Obtain	125
Chapter 17 — Visualize	135
Chapter 18 — Embrace & Enjoy	143
Chapter 19 — Reclaim	155
Chapter 20 — Financial Abundance	161
Chapter 21 — Closing Thoughts	169
Next Steps	175
References	177
The Author	185

Scan to download the Success Activity Workbook!

Foreword

In 2019, a likeable American with a winning smile and a New York accent unexpectedly popped up on a Zoom call. The man was Martin Salama, and at the time, I had no idea that our paths would cross many times over the years to come. Little did I know that this chance encounter would blossom into an enduring and inspiring friendship.

Martin has taken every coaching program I have offered, proving to be an engaged, willing, and valuable participant in each one. Like a sponge, he absorbs every piece of knowledge, experience, and advice with eagerness and enthusiasm, possessing an almost photographic memory for quotes, gems of wisdom, and sage advice.

That's why it is so startling to hear life hasn't always been a bed of roses for him.

In Worrier to Warrior, Martin offers readers an intimate glimpse into his own journey of transformation, sharing not only his wisdom but also his vulnerabilities. Like so many of us, he has experienced great struggle – experiencing tragedy, broken relationships, and shattered finances – but ultimately excelling in the face of great adversity. Martin has most certainly 'walked the walk'.

Martin's life-changing philosophy teaches us how to live by the acronym L.I.F.E (Living Incredibly Full Everyday). In a world that often postpones happiness for future milestones, embracing the present and living fully each day is a timely and sage message for today's harried souls.

What Martin conveys so powerfully is the truth that living a full or a lacklustre life is a choice. Instead of prescribing a rigid path or a one-size-fits-all solution, he demonstrates that, in any given moment, we have options in how we respond to situations.

We don't have to react with anger, fear or negativity. We are not powerless in the face of suffering. Far from it. We have choices, and those choices shape our lives.

That knowledge alone could change a life. It could change your life.

While the title may suggest a battle, this book is not about fighting but choosing. As Martin explains, it's not our successes but our reactions to struggles that make all the difference. How we recover from adversities is what makes us warriors.

I think what sets Martin apart from so many other self-improvement authors is his relatable, conversational writing style. Reading this book feels as easy as having a chat with a dear friend. His good humour and infectious enthusiasm shine through on every page, making you smile, laugh, and nod in agreement. The narrative is sprinkled with anecdotes and personal experiences that both illustrate his points and keep us engaged from start to finish.

This is a book for ordinary people, for those who prefer straightforward language to flowery esoteric prose. Martin connects with the average man and woman, reaching out to those who pause to wonder, 'What can I do to improve my life?'

Perhaps my greatest personal takeaway from Worrier to Warrior was Martin's suggestion that we reframe 'I can't' as 'I choose not to'. What a difference that makes! It takes the disempowering 'I can't' and transforms it into a conscious empowering choice. This one little move alone could result in a spectacular improvement in one's overall success and wellbeing.

Martin brings humour, charm, and down-to-earth grit to the world of self-improvement. This isn't just a business for him; it's a passion. When he showed me an early version of his book, I told him he had enough material for six books! I couldn't be more delighted to see that he took my advice, refined his work, and prepared this remarkable book for the world.

After reading Worrier to Warrior, I think you'll agree with me that Martin is like a breath of fresh, honest air, a man of extreme integrity who seeks the truth in all things. The book is ultimately a testament to the resilience of the human spirit and the immeasurably transformative power of taking life into one's own hands.

Genevieve Davis, author of Becoming Magic
Hove, UK

"Life offers neither problems nor challenges, only opportunities."

Unknown

Introduction

Welcome to The Worrier to Warrior book! Congratulations on taking that first step in creating your own Warrior's L.I.F.E. Code so you can Live Incredibly Full Everyday!

I'm excited for you! By reading this book, you're committing to your success and growth. The adage "you reap what you sow" can be applied here. The more you commit to your success, the more successful you will be.

We each define success differently, and your journey is like no one else's. Keep an open mind, and trust yourself and me along the way. Your decision today will pave the way for you to have everything you want in your LIFE. Remember: you must surrender to the process to accomplish your goals in this journey.

Divorce as a Grueling Catalyst:
My Transformation Story

Before we begin, I'd like to tell you how I got to be here, right now with you, reading this book.

Let's go back to something life-changing that happened when I was ten. I'm walking home from school with one of my four older sisters. As we get closer to our house, I see a school bus parked on the street in front of our house. I hear screaming. Then my mother comes out of the house holding my five-year-old brother Michael and runs to her car. I found out later that when my brother got off the bus, he dropped something on the road in front of the bus and crouched down to pick it up. The bus driver didn't see him, drove, and hit him.

Four days later, Michael succumbed to his injuries and passed away. This event was a defining moment for me. It was the most terrible day of my life, and I have re-lived it countless times. It was then that I created this story in my head that because of now being the only son in the family, I needed to make my parents happy always, no matter what. So, I made many decisions in my life based on trying to make them happy.

As I grew up, that theme continued in my life over and over. I have always felt the need to please loved ones and keep them happy at any expense. Usually, it was at my expense. The one person I was not concerned about making happy was myself. Even then, I usually didn't make anyone else happy, either. Often, I compromised my values at the expense of what I thought was "the bigger picture."

After I married, this got even worse. Not only did I believe I had to make my parents happy, but I also had to make my wife happy! Simultaneously spinning all these plates was exhausting, but I rationalized that it was all for the greater good, as it brought what I perceived as peace and harmony within my family unit. But nothing could have been further from the truth! No one was ever happy, and I eventually learned that "rationalize" means "rational lies." Let that sink in.

Whenever you do something against your values, you will rationalize all the reasons why it's okay. But you're really lying to yourself that it's rational to think that. In my case, I found I was fooling myself by saying that everything was great when the truth was everything was terrible. My need to please everyone ended up pleasing no one. Living up to the expectations and values of others ignores our own unique stories and inner worlds. Later I realized the only life I could be responsible for was my own.

The recurring theme in my marriage was that even when I wanted to say no to my wife, I would eventually give in, whatever the outcome. I didn't understand how I constantly betrayed my values by not standing up for what I believed so I wouldn't "make waves." Looking back, I can easily blame her. I always had the power to say no, but my confidence was so low, and I was so afraid of losing her love that I would say yes to make her happy—or so I thought.

For example, even though I believe family is important, I sometimes allowed my wife's priorities to dictate whether I visited my parents and sisters on holidays. Looking back, I've realized that reasons are often nothing more than disguised excuses that I rationalized as true.

Even when rationalizing, things don't always go as planned. When I got married, I believed it was forever. On our 24th anniversary, my wife asked for a divorce. I felt many emotions: anger, fear, shame, and loneliness. I felt like my world was crashing down around me. I moved out of our house in New Jersey and back to my childhood neighborhood in Brooklyn, New York.

The divorce was finalized a year later. I decided it was time to reflect on my life and reinvent myself. I started this process by looking deep within myself and figuring out what I liked to do and how I could make a career out of it. I recognized the thing I wanted to do most was help people. Growing up, I was always involved in outreach organizations and was a leader in my community. In that role, I enjoyed helping people realize their potential. As I looked at different careers, I found life coaches had many of the same qualities—empathy, intuition, listening, and cheerleading, to name a few.

So, I decided to become a life coach. A life coach is a certified professional who helps clients set and achieve personal goals. Life coaches do this by listening carefully, asking great questions, expanding the client's picture of what they can achieve, and collaborating with the client to set up support structures and systems to achieve their goals.

When I started my coaching training, I didn't know what I wanted my focus to be. Attending coaching school while going through my divorce helped me focus my coaching on the niche of divorce recovery.

Recovering from the divorce wasn't easy. I learned a lot about myself and the areas I needed to improve, such as my temper, self-esteem, and ability to rationalize and blame everyone else for my problems. Looking back now, despite the pain I felt at the time, I wouldn't change a thing. I'm the man I am today and can help you with your growth because I experienced the growth myself. I accomplished my healing process by understanding who I was before and who I was becoming.

Each person's process is different, and how you recover is up to you; it's your choice. What's great about working with a coach is that coaches help to expedite the healing process.

I've put the pain of the past behind me. I no longer feel anger toward my ex-wife; as a matter of fact, we have an open line of communication regarding our children. My self-confidence has dramatically increased, and now I have a great relationship with my kids.

As a result of my journey, in June 2018, with a new sense of self-worth, I got married to the most incredible woman. I discovered a vision for my life by shifting my mindset to the important things. I wanted to move forward and live a happy, joyful life. I have taken a new paradigm shift and created a program around this concept called The Warrior's L.I.F.E. Code. The acronym stands for "Live Incredibly Full Everyday!"

I'm excited to help you through growing in this process as well! As you take this journey, the emotional pain you feel will lift, and you will feel like you can be happy again, that you can start all over again, and that you can let go of the past. You can feel like it's okay to live for today.

Being told change is possible isn't enough; change also takes action. I've included Success Activities throughout the book to ensure you have somewhere to start in taking action to make the change you want to see in your LIFE. Each exercise should take around 15 minutes. If it takes longer, take a breath, and remember to listen to your true, instinctual desires! The purpose of the activities is to help you move past the noise of overthinking and get to the root of what you truly desire.

Now, there will be times that you are going to have to stretch yourself, dig deep inside, and get uncomfortable. You're not pushing yourself if you don't get uncomfortable. The change you're looking for won't manifest if you don't push yourself out of the habits and patterns that are keeping you in your current state.

While it might be harsh for me to say that, would you rather I join your pity party and let you wallow in your self-doubt or misery? Or do you want me to be your accountability partner and cheerleader? That's what I thought—you want growth and abundance in your life! That's why I'm going to help you train your inner warrior!

Keep your progress moving, and start with your first activity by reading through the activity instructions on the next page and then downloading the workbook using the QR code on the Table of Contents page.

TIP!

On the Table of Contents page, there is a QR Code to download the entire Success Activity Workbook to follow along with the activities that appear throughout this book.

Success Activity 1a

> Write down your number one reason for picking up this book. Then write down the number one goal you want to achieve by the time you reach the last page.

Success Activity 1b

> Complete the "Commitment Contract." This contract affirms your commitment to the process and playing full out, doing everything required to Live Incredibly Full Everyday! It's important to create buy-in to keep the momentum even during the difficult periods of this process.

PART 1:
TOOLS FOR SUCCESS

"The great secret of getting what you want from life is to know what you want and believe you can have it."

Norman Vincent Peale

Chapter 1 — Admission, Cleansing & Celebration

> "The best way to say 'Thank you, God' is by letting go of the past and living in the present moment."
>
> *Don Miguel Ruiz*

> "Yesterday is history. Tomorrow's a mystery. Today is a gift, and that's why it's called the present."
>
> *Alice Morse Earle*

In this first chapter, we begin down the road to uncovering your greatness with three steps:

- Admission (understanding where you came from).
- Cleansing (assessing where you are right now).
- Celebration (identifying where you want to go).

Stepping through this progression is an essential part of the healing process.

Let's take a look at these three steps in detail.

Admission

The first element is acknowledging that the way you live now is not working. Once you've made this declaration to yourself, you no longer have to look back and try to figure out what went wrong or how you can fix the past. You declare that you are ready to move on with your life, which frees you up to begin the process of cleansing. If you're struggling with this, don't worry; I'll show you how you can get there.

Cleansing

After you have admitted you need a change, it's time to let go of the feelings holding you back. Feelings like anger, frustration, dejection, and sadness don't serve you; they only hurt you and those around you. Cleansing those feelings will set you free to move forward in your life without looking in the rear-view mirror. Again, we'll step through this process together.

Celebration

With steps 1 and 2 behind you, it's time to begin enjoying your new life. But just thinking about it isn't enough; physically rejoicing allows you to proclaim to yourself and the world that you are free from the past and the people who made you miserable. So go out and have a party, dance, have fun, and spend time with those who appreciate this new you. Do whatever allows you to delight in your new life. It's a beautiful place to be.

I know it's hard to believe that happiness and success are possible. I understand how you feel; I felt the same way. If you're willing to put in the effort, I'm here to tell you there's a light at the end of the tunnel.

Here's an example from my journey. As I've said before, I went through coach training while I was getting divorced. It was God's way of telling me I would get through this.

My admission step involved facing the fact that no matter how much I didn't want to get divorced, it was happening. My marriage was over, and the situation was out of my control. This last part was huge since I was a big control freak.

My cleansing happened as I understood that several default personality traits were not serving me. My short temper, my need to control everything, and my habit of taking everything personally were just a few. I decided to accept my identity and, more importantly, commit to changing those negative traits.

Applying the lessons I learned in coaching school to my life, I completely transformed into the person I wanted to be. I often refer to my old self as Martin 1.0 and my new self as Martin 2.0. I am so much happier being Martin 2.0!

For me, the celebration step began the day I could look at myself in the mirror and not only like who I saw—but also love him. Getting myself to that point didn't happen overnight. It involved a gradual shift in my mindset and belief in myself.

I realized I had accomplished that feat when I told the amazing woman I had been dating for only one month that I wanted to tell her something and didn't need to hear it back. Then I told her I loved her. My desire to tell her grew when I realized I could love and be loved for who I was.

I didn't need to hear her say "I love you" because I was happy with who I was. And I wanted to tell the person who made me feel this way that she was the source of that happiness. Soon after, to my delight, she told me she loved me, too, and two years later, I married her. As of this writing, Sarita and I have been happily married for five years.

Now, the celebration step happens every morning when I wake up and thank God for who I have become and for the opportunity to help others to Live Incredibly Full Everyday!

Success Activity 2a

Write down the things you feel you need to change as you progress through admission, cleansing, and celebration.

Success Activity 2b

Revisit your reason for reading this book that you wrote down in Activity 1. Don't be afraid to dig deeper into your original answers to these questions. The more honest you are with yourself, the more you'll be able to clearly identify the changes you need to make moving forward.

"If it is to be, it is up to me."

William H. Johnson

Chapter 2 —
Origins of The Warrior's L.I.F.E. Code

What is The Warrior's L.I.F.E. Code?

I'd like to tell you how The Warrior's L.I.F.E. Code came about. I created it after realizing how well I had progressed post-divorce once I let go of all the negative feelings holding me back.

For me, that process began about three years after my divorce. While I had done a great job moving past the divorce, I still had areas to work on—most pressing, my health and weight.

I was moonlighting as a divorce-focused life coach while spinning my wheels, working at a dead-end job by day. My life coach training heightened my self-awareness, so I knew I was making self-destructive health and lifestyle choices. I rationalized (again, rational lies) that I was stuck in an unhappy job, and that my efforts to grow my coaching business were going almost nowhere. I wasn't yet fully willing to take full responsibility, and I had allowed my weight to balloon to an all-time high of 229 pounds!

One morning, a friend and I were walking home from daily services at my synagogue. When I got to my house, I tripped on the stairs, stumbled forward, and flew into the stucco-covered wall. My friend, who had continued walking, ran back to see what had happened. He said, "Are you alright? It sounded like an earthquake!" I had bruised and badly scraped my whole right arm. Embarrassed, I said I was fine and quickly slipped into my house.

I immediately got into the shower to wash the blood from the massive scrape on my arm. I looked up and said, "Ok, God—I get the message."

I had seen a friend's Facebook post about a 25-minute daily home workout video program he was doing that had helped him succeed in his weight loss journey. The short from-home format appealed to me because I didn't have time to go to the gym, but I could wake up about a half-hour earlier to get in the 25-minute workouts. So I contacted my friend, asked him some questions, and finally decided to make changes. This one decision has had a profound impact on my life!

In my book *Recovering From Divorce*, I talk about defining moments in our lives.[1] Often it's not until some time later that we realize we've lived through one or more of these defining moments. As I looked back later, I realized surrendering to God that I was not making the right choices in my life was one of these defining moments for me.

I'll be honest: it was rough when I first started exercising! I struggled even to do the moderated versions of the exercises, vomiting multiple times during the first two weeks. But the scrapes and bruises were constant reminders of why I was doing this. In a short time, I was feeling better and seeing results. This one decision led me to lose 65 pounds in nine months! And it did so much more.

Something happens when you start a consistent exercise program. The endorphins you produce give you more energy, more desire to exercise, and many other benefits. Speaking only for myself, I can confirm this phenomenon: As I started to see the weight loss, I began to feel better about myself. My mindset slowly started shifting from that of a complaining victim experiencing personal conflict and lack to a self-responsible warrior, practicing gratitude and abundance.

I started writing a daily list of things I was grateful for. I read self-help books. I even occasionally meditated. Over time, I experienced a total transformation—from an unhappy, self-loathing person going through a divorce to a man who liked and eventually loved himself. I was ready to start dating, with the mindset of finding someone to love and, just as importantly, finding someone who would love me for me—with neither of us trying to change the other and both of us reveling in the joy of being together—no more, no less.

One day while attempting a ten-minute guided meditation (a previously hopeless endeavor for a fidgety guy with a racing brain), I had a massive download of information, thoughts, and ideas. After I finished, I pulled out a legal pad and wrote for more than two hours. That day I wrote the framework for what has become The Warrior's L.I.F.E. Code.

That day, I came up with the acronym L.I.F.E.—"Live Incredibly Full Everyday." In that brief stretch of "meditating," I had an A.H.A. moment! I realized how happy I was, having shifted my mindset to recognize that it's up to me to design my life the way I want to live it! No matter my financial, physical, emotional, mental, spiritual, professional, or personal status, how I look at things makes all the difference in the world. So I decided that day—that moment—that I would Live Incredibly Full Everyday!

So why "The Warrior's L.I.F.E. Code"?

Everyone has faced adversity in their life. Some of the significant transformative moments in my life include:
- My brother Michael died when I was 10.
- I lost everything in the financial crash of 2008.
- My wife asked for a divorce on our 24th anniversary, a year and a half later.

You've had your moments as well. How you recover from those adversities is what makes you a warrior.

Warriors not only recover from adversity and survive, but they also UNCOVER their greatness and thrive.

The Warrior's L.I.F.E. Code combines the warrior archetype with the L.I.F.E. philosophy! I'm delighted to help you put it into practice. As the architect of The Warrior's L.I.F.E. Code, I can help you quickly shift your mindset and UNCOVER your greatness so you, too, can Live Incredibly Full Everyday!

Chapter 3 — Success Stories

Making progress can be challenging when you haven't defined the change you want to create. I'd like to show you a few success stories from clients I have worked with, so you can see the change you can accomplish in your LIFE. I'll also include my story about the changes I have seen over more than a decade so you can see what to expect long-term from your journey.

A question is likely circulating in your mind: Can I do this? I can confidently say YES, you can! If you follow the steps in this book, allow yourself to surrender to the process and do the activities, you'll see anything you want is possible, as long as you don't hold back, make assumptions, or rationalize (or as I like to say, use Rational Lies).

Here are some success stories to inspire you and give you an idea of the possibilities for you:

Client Story 1

Roberta reached out to me during a challenging time. She had lost her six-figure job due to COVID, was very depressed, and felt very lost. She had no idea what she wanted to do next in her career since she had already attained her dream job. In her words, "Martin was very empathetic and helped me come out of the hole I felt I was in with guiding questions, encouragement, and accountability. Within a couple of months, I had direction, focus, and renewed energy around all the possibilities I could now pursue. Thank you, Martin, for helping me get back on track with LIFE!"

Roberta felt like the world was falling apart right around her, and she needed reassurance and a certain amount of hand-holding to let her know that her future was in her hands. After coaching with me for a few months, she partnered with a colleague and started a new business doing what she loves. We check in periodically, and I'm happy to report she is happy, successful, and optimistic that the future holds whatever it is she wants in her life!

Client Story 2

Another of my clients, Josh, was ready to give up all hope of having a happy life when he started with The Warrior's L.I.F.E. Code program. He thought this was his last shot and that if this didn't work, he would give up and become a tool for other people's happiness. He didn't understand that his internal limiting beliefs and rational lies kept him tied to his old way of thinking.

Since starting the program with me, he has gained positive clarity. He has accepted his power and choice. He has taken responsibility for his choices and let go of those that were not his. He has decided to live in abundance and gratitude.

He says, "Because of those changes that Martin taught me, I am happier, I have better relationships, and I have more clients because I am being my real, positive self. Looking back, all I wanted was hope that I could start to heal. Needless to say, I have it now."

As a coach, I could not be happier for Roberta and Josh. They have come to understand with the right coaching and willingness to be open-minded, they can change their mindset of lack to one of abundance, gratitude, and joy!

My Journey

In the first few chapters of this book, you've read about how devastated I was when my wife asked me for a divorce on our 24th anniversary. I tried everything I could to convince her to stay with me.

The real reason I wanted to stay married, I came to understand later, was all about me: my lack of self-confidence, self-love, and self-worth. I needed to consider who I was, who I wanted to be, and most importantly, why! In the beginning, I was afraid no one would ever love me, and I figured the best hope I had was to get the woman who once loved me to love me again. But the truth is she was right: I was a control freak, I took everything personally, and I had such a bad temper that when I reacted to a situation, I was like a Nuclear Reactor! Leaving fall-out all over that I needed to go back and clean up. I can look back now and say this was a defining moment that changed my life forever and in a good way. She gave me the proverbial kick in the pants that I needed to make lasting changes in my L.I.F.E.

That first step was scary, especially since I didn't want to take it. But what were my choices? Curl up in a ball and throw a pity party? Beg her to try again, with no real change in either of us? We were in a very codependent relationship. My lifelong need to please everyone, especially her, was toxic for both of us and the kids.

In retrospect, we were both responsible parties and victims in the relationship. I took stock of myself and decided I needed to make some changes in my life. Not for her or to get her back, not for the kids, only for me. If I did it for any other reason, the changes would be temporary. Instead, I chose lasting change, and as a result, I am a completely different person than I was. So much so that I call my old self Martin 1.0 and my new self Martin 2.0.

Do you want the same for yourself? Do you want to transform your L.I.F.E. and how you interact with yourself and those around you? What was your defining moment or aha moment that kindled your determination to make this change? Maybe you've also experienced divorce, weight struggles, or the death of a loved one. Perhaps it's something entirely different for you. We each have our path and experiences. I believe it's important to reflect on these defining moments and do a deep dive to clarify how they have affected us and how we need to heal from them.

Let me be clear: I'm telling you to do this, not so you become stuck in thinking about the past. Not at all. It's just the opposite, so you can put it into perspective and let it serve and help you heal. It's about recognizing the past's effect on your life, both good and bad, and allowing yourself to move forward. Use the following Success Activity to help you with this.

Success Activity 3a

> Use the activity sheet to answer questions about your past defining moments. Take as long as you'd like and write as much as you feel you need to. Think deeply about what you want to write. As I said earlier, admission is the first step in the process to UNCOVER the greatness within you.

TIP!

By acknowledging and admitting it, you're starting down the path to the happiness, joy, and L.I.F.E. you want so you can Live Incredibly Full Everyday!

Success Activity 3b

> Next, write down what your new L.I.F.E. looks like. Be specific. I mean very specific. I want you to create a vision board, with pictures and descriptions of what your L.I.F.E. looks like.

Remember when writing out your defining moments that these don't define you unless you let them; they can only define you with your permission. Those past moments can hold you back with chains of anger, resentment, and regret, or they can propel you to commemorate, reflect, and appreciate. This entire process is about your choice and recognizing you always have the power to choose.

So now, let's take what you wrote down about who you are now, the things you like about yourself, and the things you don't like. Your vision board will help you define the change you want to see.

For my vision boards, I love to use a program called Canva. Take a look at an early version of my vision board (available to view through the QR code on the Table of Contents page). I say early because it's an ever-changing, ever-evolving idea board. As I reach one of my goals, I update it.

One of the biggest reasons I see others miss goals is they don't have a personalized reminder of why they want to reach their goal. Regularly reviewing and updating your vision board takes this pitfall out of the equation. Review your board frequently to help you visualize achieving your goal!

So what will be represented on your vision board? Will it have the amount of money you want to make this year? Will it have pictures of places you want to visit? Will it have things you want to accomplish? Family pictures?

What you're putting on this vision board is your WHY. Your WHY is probably the most important reason you're doing any of this.

Here's another acronym: WHY Stands for "What's Hurting You?" What deep within you bothers or hurts you so much that you're willing to put in the work to change it?

As you create your vision board, keep your WHY in mind to guide, inspire, motivate, and get what you want.

Chapter 4 —
The Cycle of A's (Ask, Act, Attitude)

In this chapter, I'm going to tell you something that sounds like it contradicts what we've discussed up to this point. In the last chapter, we discussed the vision board and your WHY - What's Hurting You?

Your vision board shows what you want and are working towards; it doesn't actively change where you're at—that's where these next steps come in.

I don't want you to attach too much desire to what you show on your vision board as what you want. If there's too much desire, you'll experience lack instead of abundance. I'll go deeper into this later. For now, let's focus on creating what you want by asking the universe for it. We'll also discuss acting upon it by putting in the effort.

The next step is the one that looks like a contradiction; do not attach any emotion to whatever outcome happens. It's part of the process. You may not get what you want. You may get the exact opposite. That's ok; it's just a bump in the road. It's the universe telling you not to put emotion behind the outcome. Let it go and let it happen in time. Don't get me wrong, detaching emotion from the outcome is tough. Your inner voice will push you to feel desire and want—that's lack! The more you put emotion behind it, the harder it will be to attain it. Let me explain why.

The first step is understanding the Law of Attraction and how to use it. Asking the universe for what you want is not enough. The universe isn't Santa Claus. How do you expect anything to happen if you ask for what you want and take no action toward it? If you aren't putting any energy into the action, why should the universe?

The nuance comes here: If you take action toward what you want but put too much desire towards it, the universe sees the desire as an attitude of lack. The attitude of lack will keep you away from attaining what you want. The balance occurs when you take action but allow the universe to work out the details—allowing changes to unfold without becoming distressed or micromanaging how the universe works to bring you what you desire. This technique is one I initially learned from one of my mentors, Genevieve Davis; I've slightly modified it here as I have effectively incorporated it into my life.[1]

It's a cycle of perpetual motion. Each part of the cycle must be active to manifest what you want fully. One leads into the next, which leads into the next. In the beginning, you'll start with Ask, move on to Act and come to Attitude. As you build self-confidence in this cycle, they intertwine and work symbiotically.

So let's practice setting up a cycle: Ask, Act, Attitude.

The Ask step is where the concept of the Law of Attraction comes into play. You may have never even heard of the Law of Attraction or may not fully understand how it works, but you're still living by its laws; because it's a Universal Law that operates in our lives, every minute of every day.

The Law of Attraction, as defined simply by Michael Losier in his book *Law of Attraction*, is: I attract to my life whatever I give my energy, focus, and attention to, whether wanted or unwanted.[2] The entire point of this step is to Ask the Universe,

God, or your Higher Power for what you want. That's all you need to do for this step!

It's important to remember: Our feelings and moods emit vibrations (positively or negatively, high or low frequency) that draw us to people, places, things, and events that match the vibrations we're emitting.

At every moment, I offer a positive or negative vibration. At every moment, the Law of Attraction responds to that vibration, giving me more of the same, whether wanted or unwanted. This passive attraction is called Non-deliberate Attraction.

For example, you give attention to what you don't want when you use the words "DON'T, NOT, or NO." When you use these words, immediately stop and say, "What DO I want?" If I fail to get clear about what I DO want, according to the Law of Attraction, I will attract that which I don't want in my life, again and again—until I place my focus on something else.

If you are curious about your vibration level, observe what's showing up in your life. It's a perfect match and will tell you where you might want to adjust your vibration to attract your desired results and circumstances.

The Law of Attraction responds powerfully to energy, meaning it responds to how you *feel* about what you say and what you think. John Assaraf stated this concept succinctly when he said, "When we have opposing energies, they cancel each other out. Yes, get the mindset and vision right, but also get the emotions right. Get in coherence with the feeling—the energy in motion."[3] Change your vibration, change your results.

Ask is the first step, but there is more you need to do after asking for what you want. After you've clarified what you want to Ask, it's time to move on to the next step: Act.

Here's where I believe the next steps in the Cycle become vital. It's about creation in addition to manifestation. In the basic sense of The Law of Attraction, this is where the foundation of asking for what you want is not enough. Manifestation means expecting something to happen just because you asked. As I said, that's a fundamental concept of The Law of Attraction, where many people get stuck. When things don't happen as expected, they lose faith and give up, blaming it on the fact that The Law of Attraction doesn't work. They rationalize, "It's not me; it's the concept."

On the one hand, you're right because The Law of Attraction says: ask, think, want, and it will come. On the other hand, however, this thinking is inaccurate because without action, how can you expect anything to change?

The Act step is where you begin taking action and moving toward what you want. Start doing things to move you closer to your goals. Move out of your comfort zone. Move in the direction of your dreams.

It's vital at this juncture to detach expectation from what begins happening. Once you begin taking action, things will start to change. Sometimes the changes that occur will be what you want, and you'll feel great about where everything is leading! Other times, however, things may look precisely opposite the way you wanted them to. Remember that just because the outcome wasn't what you wanted, it may be something that needed to happen along the way to get you to your goals.

Here's where your faith has to be strong and accept the process. Along the way, things will happen that you may want to dismiss as a coincidence. Every little thing counts, regardless of whether it looks good or bad; everything that happens plays a part in some way. When these things happen, remind yourself the universe is doing what is needed to help you on your journey. It may not look at the time like what you want, but take a minute to reflect on what happened and then continue your journey.

The last step, Attitude (or letting go of the results), is usually the most challenging step of the cycle. It's hard-wired into your nature to have an emotional response about the outcomes you experience. Here is where it pays off to release attachments to specific outcomes. The more emotion and attention you devote to the outcome, the more you operate from a place of lacking the thing you are working to achieve. Rather than moving toward what you want to achieve, your attention on not having the results already in your life will derail your efforts and cause those results to move further away. In short, the more "lack" you operate in, the more what you want to achieve will elude you.

This step can be difficult because it involves releasing those feelings of want. You're likely saying, "Martin, I can't do that!" I know how you feel! It's understandable because that's what you've been taught and what you've believed your whole life. I felt the same way. Do you know what I found? The more I let go of the emotion of the outcome, the more quickly I could achieve my goals.

As things happened (especially the negative), diverting me from my goal, I began to realize there's a reason for everything. These moments signaled that it was time for me to review, reflect and adjust without getting emotional about these "bumps in the road." More often than not, I found those "bumps" were telling me something. By not getting emotionally attached to the outcome, I could see the good that resulted from the "bad" thing that happened. As I released control, the universe gave me the necessary course correction toward my ultimate goal.

Genevieve Davis, calls the entire process "Magic" and the idea that when anything happens to you, it's not through coincidence.[1] Anything "good" or "bad" that happens is magic you manifest and create in your L.I.F.E. Your attitude and mindset toward what you want to determine the outcome. The more you worry, feel anxious, and react toward what you want, the more it won't come.

The more you release worry and begin to accept and respond, the more it attracts to you—like a magnet attracting iron filings. It will feel like magic, and you might say, "This is a one-off! A coincidence!" At those moments, surrender to the attitude that it's Magic! Recognize it, appreciate it, act upon it, build on it, and continue to let go of the results.

Remember, this is a cycle of perpetual motion, so it's best to shift your mindset to being in Ask, Act, and Attitude at all times.

Success Activity 4a

> Take a look at the Cycle of A's in the Activity Book. Think of a change you want to manifest and create in your L.I.F.E. and use the activity sheet to break it into steps for Ask, Act, and Attitude.

Success Activity 4b

> As you move toward your goals, take time to review, reflect and adjust your course of action without getting emotionally attached to the outcome. Continue this evaluation throughout the process to keep yourself moving forward and on track!

TIP!

Start with something easy and build from there. You can always come back and download another copy for something else you want to put through the cycle.

Before we go any further, I want to say congratulations! You made it through Part 1! You are well on your way to developing your own Warrior's L.I.F.E. Code. Remember to celebrate each of your wins as you continue through the book. Every step forward is progress and deserves acknowledgment and celebration.

So how are you feeling after going through these last chapters? Do you see the light at the end of the tunnel? If so, great! If not, don't worry; it will happen as you continue practicing the steps we've discussed.

Remember that this is a journey full of many small steps. I tell my clients that any quick, overwhelming changes are not sustainable. The most lasting changes are those that happen over time. As you digest this information and put what we're discussing into practice, you will see incremental changes begin to occur.

I have a recommendation for you to keep in mind as you move through this process. Don't proclaim to the people in your world, "Wait until you see the new me." Nobody wants to hear what you're saying—they want to see what you're doing.

Make changes for yourself, and as those changes start to take hold and become part of the new you, everyone around you will notice the changes. They'll also appreciate that you're not engaging in some of your old habits—like getting in their face about the changes you're making. In the past, you may have said, "You see, I'm not doing so and so anymore." That's precisely what you don't want to do now. You want them to figure it out on their own. If you point it out to them, you're probably doing it for the wrong reason. If they notice on their own, it means they recognize the changes and are beginning to appreciate them.

If you want to create a mindset of abundance, it means taking a leap of faith. Trust the process, trust me and, more importantly, trust yourself. Keep in mind you're doing this so you can Enjoy L.I.F.E. and Live Incredibly Full Everyday!

Start shifting your mindset right now! Begin each morning by expressing gratitude to your higher power (God, the universe, whatever it is)! I use this technique every morning to focus on the good in the day ahead. As you move through your day, continue expressing gratitude for all of the good things in your L.I.F.E. and say to yourself, "I'm going to Live Incredibly Full Everyday!" Get into the habit of doing it every morning at the very minimum.

Now it's time to buckle up! These last chapters were easy tips to get you started. In Part 2, I'll take you through practical steps that will take you deeper into the changes you're starting here. The changes will start out looking small, but you'll begin to understand how powerful these techniques are as you continue using them.

Remember, this is about who you want to be from here on out.

PART 2: DEEP DIVE INTO TRANSFORMATION

"When you define another, you do not define them, you define yourself."

Wayne Dyer

Chapter 5 — Stop

Before we dive deep into this following process, let's go back to my story for a minute. For me, recovering from the divorce wasn't easy. I learned a lot about myself and the areas I needed to improve, like my temper, self-esteem, and tendency to rationalize and blame everyone else for my problems. Looking back now at how I've changed and what I've learned, I wouldn't change a thing.

Each person's process is different, and it's your choice how you use the UNCOVER process. A bonus you have, though, is you can move through this process faster than I did because you have all the tools in one place! I made it through the healing process by understanding who I was when I started and who I wanted to be, followed by a lot of trial and error.

As you take this journey, your mindset will shift, and you will UNCOVER your greatness so you can be truly happy, letting go of fear and lack to make way for abundance and joy. By allowing this process to set you free, you can begin to enjoy L.I.F.E. and Live Incredibly Full Everyday!

Shifting your mindset requires you to find a new way of looking at things. An easy way to accomplish this mindset shift is to transform your daily interactions with others. Your mindset will gradually shift as you have increasingly more successful interactions with those around you. To help you experience this mindset shift, I developed three steps that will help you improve any interaction. Let's get into it now.

Remember when you were a kid in school, and the local fire department would come into the class to talk about fire safety? That was a while ago, but I still remember the firefighter talking about the steps to take if you are near a flame and your clothes catch fire: Stop, Drop, and Roll. Stop where you are so you don't spread the fire by moving around, Drop to the ground, and Roll until the flame has been smothered. These simple guidelines are easy to remember and will stick with you forever.

Life presents situations where a similar emergency protocol can be applied. Questions, decisions, and conversations come at us from left and right every day. Whether they are regarding relationships, health, career, or finances, we have daily opportunities to make decisions. It can sometimes feel like we're on fire in uncomfortable situations. These situations are why I created an easy-to-remember, three-step process to handle these and "put out" the situational fires you are experiencing.

These situational fires can be anything:
- A financial opportunity presents itself, and you need help figuring out what to do.
- It's the perfect time of day to exercise, but you don't feel fired up to go to the gym.
- Your partner starts getting on your nerves after a long day at work.
- Your boss offers a promotion with better pay but longer hours, and you need help deciding.
- Or the most probable scenario: You face an uncomfortable position, like an argument, and you want to get out of some negative and possibly even highly charged situations.

To address these situations, I took Stop, Drop & Roll and changed it to Stop, Think & Respond.

Before we get into Step 1, I'd like to tell you a story about when I learned to practice Stop, Think, and Respond.

In 2008, I lost every penny I had due to the recession. I lost both my money and millions of dollars of my family's and investors' money. I was in such deep debt family members had to step in and take over my finances and set up a budget for me, my wife, and my family. I had to account for every dollar spent of the money coming in, which, at that time, was real estate income.

A large part of the money coming in went right back out to pay back vendors from my daughter's wedding, which happened just as everything fell apart. Eventually, I even lost the real estate income when I had to repay the family losses after the dust from the financial fallout settled. These circumstances understandably put me into depression—so much so that I was prescribed Wellbutrin, an antidepressant.

I was on Wellbutrin for over eight months, but since my finances were in such disarray, I allowed my health insurance to lapse. As a result, I couldn't afford any more medication after eight months. I started wondering what to do. I believed the pills were working, but I was also beginning to think that my depression was self-inflicted. Clinically it was called situational depression—also called "stress response syndrome."

I thought about everything that had happened to me and what I could do to turn things around. I felt that, in this case, the dependence on the medication had more to do with my state of mind than a persistent chemical imbalance. I was allowing my circumstances to dictate my depressive reaction. At that same time, I was becoming more aware of my emotions, feelings, thoughts, and actions and how they are all deeply interconnected.

Experience has taught me that a person's self-reflection often increases when life unravels. Turbulent times push us to reconsider our actions and evaluate our approach to life. In contrast, when things are going well, you usually ride an emotional high and feel everything is great! However, you question almost everything when things aren't going well. You become introspective and ask yourself, "Why, how, when, and what now?!"

Similarly, it was during my transition off of Wellbutrin that I realized I am the master of my emotions. It took about a year or so to understand what that meant when I went through life coach training and dug deeper into the issues at play. I made a conscious decision to stop the medication and stop feeling bad for myself. I decided that my mood was all about the surrounding situation I found myself in, and it was my responsibility to, at the very least, change what I could within myself.

At first, it was a bit terrifying. Whenever I felt depressed or anxious, I was worried I would revert to depression. Then, I would take stock of myself and think about what was going on, what I felt, and what I could do differently this time. I would remind myself of the adage: it's not what happens to you; it's what you do with what's happening. Each time I began to experience symptoms of depression, my reaction would lessen. As I got better at recalibrating my emotional state, I noticed I was transforming my reactions into responses. I paid close attention to recognizing the difference and pushed myself to utilize the practice of responding as often as possible.

Let me be clear: there is a vast difference between reacting and responding. In the past, I almost always reacted. I would "shoot first and ask questions later." If you ask my ex-wife and kids, they may say I reacted so intensely that it might be more accurate to call me a "Nuclear Reactor". When I reacted, everyone in my vicinity was a fallout victim. I didn't even see it in myself until this time of change. The behavioral changes I've experienced since then are marked—another reason I refer to my old self as Martin 1.0 and my new self as Martin 2.0.

As you can see, Stop, Think, and Respond works! Now let's get into how to make this process work for you so that you can see radical changes in your L.I.F.E.!

The first step in this process is to Stop. Stop your default reaction. Stop boiling over. Reacting in that way is what got you here. The goal here is to help you communicate rather than explode. Learning to stop explosions before they begin moves you away from the behaviors that alienate those you care about.

STOP

Learn how to STOP and use clear communication and listening skills to gain control in the moment.

Disconnect from the triggers so you can listen fully. Change the way you communicate. Interrupting old patterns can make it easier to introduce new practices.

What you say is important. But how you say it is vital in getting your message across correctly and without confusion. Why is this important? Unspoken expectations of others are disappointments waiting to happen. Often, we expect someone to know exactly what we're thinking or saying when they're not clearly receiving the message we're sending. That will usually lead to disappointment from you. You may even take it out on them—thinking things like, "It's their fault, and how could they not know where I'm coming from?! They obviously don't care about me." In these moments, STOP and remember that communication is a two-way street.

Creating better communication starts by understanding, accepting, and releasing expectations. At this point, you'll be changing your habit of reacting to a practice of responding by using Step 1—Stop. As soon as you Stop before you react (or over-react), you begin defusing situations and create an opportunity for improving communication (and relationships).

In any relationship, you're bound to be disappointed when you set up expectations for someone, be it a spouse, family member, friend, co-worker, etc. The main reason is that the other person isn't aware that expectations are placed on them and are bound to fail in your eyes. Even if they do know, they cannot grasp your expectations' whole meaning. They can't live up to the unrealistic goals you set for them in your mind.

If you go into a relationship without having undue expectations from someone, your relationship can grow naturally and flow easily. Another way to look at it is to say you can't control someone else's feelings and actions. Placing expectations on someone is a way to manage them and keep them in a role you are comfortable with rather than allowing them to govern themselves.

Couples often enter marriage with expectations for the relationship that are never clearly discussed. These expectations could be as simple as the wife, who we'll call Sarah, expecting the husband, let's call him Joseph, to know he's supposed to take out the garbage when it seems full. Each time Sarah passes the overflowing pail, she gets a little more upset that Joseph hasn't changed it. On the other hand, like most men, Joseph may not even see the pail; it's as if he's blind to its existence. Meanwhile, Sarah builds up a slow burn until Joseph does something that proves to be the final straw, and an argument erupts.

Sarah's unspoken expectation that Joseph takes out the trash becomes a flashpoint while she becomes entrenched in disappointment and resentment resulting from her expectations not being met. Imagine if, earlier in the day, Sarah had clearly asked Joseph to take out the trash. He would have known she needed help, and she would have formed an accurate expectation based on his expressed willingness to help her. This way, Sarah's expectations are not left to chance and probable disappointment, and Joseph can let her know she is valued and heard.

By removing judgment, listening, and accepting the person you're interacting with as they are, you are acknowledging and validating what they are saying. Otherwise, even though you're both speaking the same language, there can be misinterpretations. One of my favorite quotes addresses this phenomenon: "What you say is about you; what I hear is about me." Meaning my perception is different from yours. Just as my circumstances impact my feelings and what I say, your life circumstances affect how you interpret what I say.

In coaching, we often talk about how thoughts lead to feelings/emotions, which lead to actions. These three aspects of your conscious and expression are intricately linked. So, imagine the possibilities if we learn how to control our feelings and what we do about them by changing our thoughts. This technique is simple, but the results are transformative.

"What you say is about you, what I hear is about me."

Unknown

Chapter 6 — Think

Learning to Stop reactions and evaluate interactions as they happen is incredibly important, but more work is needed to create lasting change. To continue this transformation, let's explore the next step, Think.

THINK

Keep these following points in mind during your interactions to get into the habit of using the first two steps, Stop and Think:
- Clear your mind, think sensibly (calmly), and take the time you need to prepare your response.
- Understand what is about you and what isn't.
- Learn how not to take things personally.
- Switch up your responses so you are responding rather than engaging in your usual reactions.

I have a bit of a self-help book habit; I can't get enough of them. One of the most personally influential books I've ever read came while training to be a life coach—*The 4 Agreements* by Miguel Ruiz.[1] I can honestly say this book changed my life. I highly recommend it. One of the Agreements is "Don't take anything personally." When I read that, it was like the tumblers of the universe clicked into place! Miguel Ruiz had revealed a secret that people had been trying to express to me for years, but until that moment, I wasn't ready to hear.

In my new state of self-awareness, I was open and actually ready to hear it. I realized that I had been taking everything that happened in the world personally my entire life. It was part of my default personality. I might not fly off the handle in public, but I would take a stand and not give an inch until everything on my mind was on the table. At home, in private, my emotions would heighten to a level that was unfair to everyone around me. I would lecture whoever didn't see my point of view until they caved from sheer exhaustion. Deep down, I justified (or rationalized) my point of view. I told myself that since the people around me knew the real me, I didn't have to put on a mask and let my guard down. Little did I know this position was cruel and abusive to those around me. Who did I think I was that I could treat my loved ones that way?

On a deep level, I was looking for acknowledgment and validation. I wanted to be in control so I felt safe. My insecurities were getting in the way of any genuine happiness. Of course, I wasn't like this all the time, but it was enough that everyone felt they had to walk on eggshells around me.

With this newfound epiphany to not take anything personally, I saw things differently; not everything was my responsibility. On a basic level, I didn't have to be a safety net for my children by getting involved in every decision they were making. I started to allow them to sink or swim on their own and wasn't attached to the outcome in any way. This shift helped me become someone they could talk to without fear of reprimand and helped my kids become more self-actualized. I had previously exerted more control for a few reasons: I didn't want them to make the same mistakes I made, and I wanted them to have a happy, blissful life with no worries. But even more importantly, I was doing what my wife wanted me to do.

If you read my first book, *Recovering From Divorce*, you'll remember I discussed my deep need for love and approval.[2] This need was so intense I would do anything my wife wanted, usually at my own cost and in violation of my values. I'm not blaming her for that; I take complete responsibility for my actions. These decisions resulted in me doing everything I could for my children to have what I considered a positive outcome. Of course, looking back, not allowing my kids to experience success or failure fully was stunting their growth and not giving them the tools to exist in the real world as adults.

On a deeper personal level, accepting Miguel Ruiz's premise not to take things personally was like having the weight of the world lifted off my shoulders. I didn't need to be in control of anything, least of all my children. It was up to them to make decisions for themselves. It took a while to grasp its meaning fully, but the world looked totally different with this new outlook.

Did the world change? The sun was still rising and setting, the people were still doing whatever they were doing before, and the politics of the day were the same as they were the day before. It became apparent I was the variable in this equation. I had changed. I was seeing everything in a new way.

The Talmud says, "We do not see the world as it is. We see it as we are." And according to Genevieve Davis, "The world is what you think it is."[3] Despite these writings being separated by thousands of years, they express the same message: Your mindset influences how you see the rest of the world.

As my mindset shifted, it was as if I was looking through a completely different viewfinder. I was seeing the same world I had been looking for decades in a completely new way. It was up to me to decide if the world around me was bright or dark, good or bad, wonderful or annoying. Recognizing why you take things personally is the first step in unwinding this response and shifting your perspective.

Now that we've explored the foundation behind Think, let's dive into the practicalities of how to apply it.

Stop and take a beat when you're in a situation that begins to escalate. However, stopping isn't enough to redirect the conversation; this is where Think becomes essential. Think about what's happening. Think about why this is affecting you. Then go deeper and evaluate if you are taking something personally or trying to justify your actions. Perhaps you feel attacked and defend yourself by reacting, overreacting, or even being a Nuclear Reactor. When you feel yourself beginning to throw up your usual walls, a crucial question to ask yourself is, "Do I feel unsafe, and am I trying to control this person or this situation?"

I know this is a lot to absorb in that split-second moment. Still, going through this step for as many interactions as possible is essential to rewrite your default reactions into responses, even during stressful interactions. Your job is to adopt the same perspective that Michael Jordan, LeBron James, Tom Brady, or any other sports figure takes into their practice sessions. They practice their moves repeatedly, so their chance of success is greater when facing a high-stakes situation on the court or field. Will they be successful every time? No! And that's okay! It's not about perfection—it's about being a better you.

You're embarking on this journey for yourself. You're practicing for you. You're becoming a better version of yourself for you. Once you have yourself taken care of, you can consider other factors: family, friends, co-workers, etc. As the saying goes, you can better help others if you put your oxygen mask on first.

The Think step isn't just for during interactions; you can also use it to review interactions and look for opportunities to improve. Let's say you couldn't implement Step 1 at that heated moment, and you went full-blown Nuclear. Afterward, take a few minutes alone to reflect on the episode and fully utilize Think.

Use this opportunity to consider what prompted the nuclear reaction. Use this as a moment of reflection to review what happened based on what you've learned thus far. Ask yourself, "What did I just do, why did I do it, what were the effects of my reaction, who did I hurt, and why?" In this moment of introspection, ask yourself the follow-up question: "How can I be better the next time?" The moment you ask yourself this question and genuinely want to find the answer is when you know change is taking root.

Moving away from reacting and toward responding takes time and practice. It's common to have many emotions and feelings bubble up during this process. Be aware this is going to happen. Be mindful of your internal state as you practice responding. The transition phase is difficult, but L.I.F.E. is much easier once you learn to respond.

When you struggle to move away from reacting, it can be helpful to have an example to emulate. Borrow inspiration from someone you admire. If you know someone who always keeps their cool, think about them when you catch yourself reacting. Take a breath, and recenter around adopting some of their energy.

Several of my clients have even come to me and reported they thought to themselves, "What would Martin do in this situation?" I even had one person say they felt like an imaginary little me was sitting on their shoulder watching their decision-making processes like the old angel and devil on the shoulder trying to convince them what they should do. Of course, for this person, it was an imaginary me on their shoulder telling them before you react - Stop. I told them, "Hey, whatever works to get you to Stop, go with it!" Eventually, this client could move forward and implement Step 1—Stop—in nearly all their interactions (including with angry customers).

Now that we have gotten a good understanding of Stop (also known as don't react) and Think (don't take things personally). The next step is to take these two steps and move on to Step 3 – Respond, which we'll do in the next chapter. ;)

"Our level of true awareness is directly related to our lack of judging."

Unknown

Chapter 7 — Respond

We've reached the third and last step in the Stop, Think, Respond approach! Let's get into how to use this step.

Step 3 - Respond - this is about changing the way you've reacted in the past, moving away from the disastrous results you used to experience, and moving toward a new way of responding for successful (and low-stress) outcomes.

RESPOND

Practice Responding Rather Than Reacting.
- Switch up how you usually engage (reacting) to break old patterns and step into new habits.
- Learn how to build bridges instead of burning them.
- Learn what you can say to be heard without creating tension.
- Show who you really want to be.

As we discussed earlier, there's a vast difference between reacting and responding. I've mentioned how in my past, I almost always reacted; I would "shoot first and ask questions later" to the point I was labeled as a "Nuclear Reactor" by my ex-wife and kids. Everyone in my vicinity was a victim of the fallout.

Here's something I haven't told you: After my divorce, when something in my teenage kids' life would happen—something that in the past I would've reacted to—they wouldn't tell me right away for fear of me blowing up based on my reactions in the past. When they finally spoke to me about issues, I would respond instead of react. Having a healthy conversation with me was so new and unexpected for my kids; they would look at me bewildered and say, "Who are you?" It took them a while to get used to the new me. It may take the people in your life some time to get used to the new you, too.

Let me give you some advice: don't point out the changes you are making to other people in your life. When your subconscious is fishing for approval and recognition for your actions, drawing attention to the changes you're making is an easy trap to fall into. Seeking external validation like this is another form of controlling others because you want them to see you're changing and to acknowledge that you're trying. Eventually, they'll see the new you and appreciate it. Just make the changes and keep going. I'm telling you this from my own experience.

A few years ago, I was interviewed as part of a compilation of short video interviews of professionals from all walks of life. They asked me about making changes in yourself and how it affects relationships with others. I answered, "Don't proclaim to the world, 'Wait until you see the new me,' because nobody wants to hear what you have to say. They want to see what you have to do." So, rather than waving it in their face, let them see the new you in their own time. Remember, your main objective, WHY you're doing this, is to be a better you for yourself first, then it's for the others in your life. Remember that you are changing these traits to be a better you—for you. If you're making changes to please others, not only will it not work long-term, but it won't be a permanent lasting change that can positively impact your life.

So how can you make this change? One of the easiest things you can do is don't react, even when you are in a typical moment of reaction (like when you're angry)! Instead, take a moment to think about what you want to say, then respond. You'll be better off. Over time, you'll learn how to control your emotions to serve you better. I'm not saying you should never get angry, but there are healthy ways of expressing anger. What you're working on now is deciding what is important to you and what response will serve you better.

Let's face it: There will be times when you get upset, and your first instinct will be to go to your default reaction. Old habits are difficult to break free from. For instance, if you're divorced with kids like me, whether you like it or not, your ex will always be your ex. They will always be part of your life in some way. While this relationship can be tricky to navigate, how you decide to relate to them is entirely up to you, not them. Your relationship with everyone outside yourself is up to you, not the other person.

In most relationships, not only in marriage but especially there, it's easy to feel like you have to answer for whatever's happening because you're shouldering the responsibility for making your partner happy, even at the cost of your happiness. Your happiness should always come first. That doesn't mean that it should be to the detriment of someone else; it only means that if you're not happy with your decisions, that will play out in many aspects of your day-to-day living. This situation is a recipe for disaster for you and the person you're trying to make happy.

Understand and accept that you choose how to show up in any relationship. No matter what games other people may try to play, how you react will decide what happens. Responding instead of reacting gives you control over your side of every interaction.

When you react and immediately get angry, upset, or excited, you're allowing your emotions to control you. When you respond, a completely different process occurs. Responding is letting whatever the other person is saying sink in and thinking about the importance of answering calmly. In this situation, you're allowing yourself to control your emotions. Again, it's not that you should never get angry; I'm just saying to pause, take stock of the situation, and measure your emotions.

Chapter 8 —
Putting It All Together

So far, we've discussed theory and the reasons behind using Stop, Think, and Respond. In this chapter, we'll learn how to use this technique so it becomes natural to you.

Before putting Stop, Think, Respond into action, let's review a few methods of dealing with conflicts.

Suffer

You can be a victim. The approach of "Everything's just going to happen to me anyway, so I'll just say whatever." I don't recommend this approach, but the decision is yours.

Accept It

You could say, "So, what?" You can ask yourself if this issue will still matter a year or even a week from now. If it doesn't matter, don't let it bother you.

Change the Situation

Do what you can to bring it closer to a resolution. This approach goes back to what we discussed before about breaking old patterns to help develop new habits.

Avoid It

You know what? You don't have to attend every argument you're invited to. It's up to you to decide whether you want to fight.

Alter the Experience

If you look at an issue differently, the experience will change. It's your world. Choose to create it as you wish. So why not alter the experience?

You can decide which method of dealing with conflict you want to use for any given situation.

Now that we have an overall understanding of your choices in a situation, let's put them together. Imagine you're in a discussion that's about to get heated. This is an opportue time to practice Stop, Think, and Respond.

Step 1 – STOP: Stop yourself from getting so upset that you're about to get into an argument. Say to yourself, is this the proper way to communicate my thoughts?

Step 2 – THINK: Think about what's going on in this situation, determine if you're starting to take it personally, and think about what you can do to diffuse this "fire" before it and you get out of control.

Step 3 – RESPOND: Instead of reacting and maybe even becoming a "Nuclear Reactor" leaving victims in your path of destruction, how about allowing the first two steps to help you respond in a way that shows who you want to be and who you know you can become.

Bruce Schneider, the founder of iPEC, the coaching school I went to, said: "Each moment describes who you are and gives you the opportunity to decide if that's who you want to be."

"It's your world; choose to create it as you wish!"

Martin Salama

Here's another quote that helped me when I was transforming myself—this one is from Eleanor Roosevelt: "No one can make you feel inferior without your consent."

It immediately became one of my favorite quotes when I heard it. Since then, I've tried to live my life by that quote. It's up to you to decide when someone puts you down how you want to feel about what they said. If you choose to allow it to affect you, it will. However, if you ignore the person's comments and accept that you are the master of your thoughts, you will be able to live a much happier life. Live life on your terms.

Here's an exercise you can use as you work on mastering your new skill. When I was a kid, there was a basketball game we used to play called 5-3-1. The game's rules were: You take a foul shot, and if you make it, you get five points. Next, you get the rebound, and wherever you are when you catch the ball, you take a shot for three points. Then you take a layup or any shot of your choosing for 1 point. If you made all three shots, you were awarded an extra point for a perfect turn to round out to ten points —the first person to one hundred points wins.

I was reminded of the game recently when my wife Sarita and my 13-year-old stepson, Ralph, went outside and played ball. When they returned, I asked them what they played and who won. They said 5-3-1, and Sarita won 100-0! I was shocked and asked how that was possible! Ralph said he kept missing the foul shot, so he kept shooting it to get 5 points to catch up instead of going for the rebound shot or layup and accumulating smaller points to at least stay in the game.

When I asked Ralph why he took this approach, he said, "I figured the bigger shots would get me there faster." I reminded him they were higher risk, and we all laughed when he said, "I figured it was worth a shot!" I pointed out he would have been better off practicing his layups and getting better with those while racking up some points. His immediate comeback was, "Nah! Go big or go home!"

While I get his reasoning, I don't always agree with it, especially in this instance. By continuing to take the big shots, he risked losing. It reminds me of the saying: I didn't become a big shot overnight; I took a lot of little shots to get here. Using Stop, Think, Respond is the same; it's a lot of little steps, practice, and getting better so you can take those big shots when they come.

We'll take the 5-3-1 example and apply it to Stop, Think, and Respond, but with a slight twist. Let's reverse the order and use 1-3-5.

As we go through this exercise, I want you to close your eyes and think about a situation where you acted in a way that produced negative results or about a situation you wish you could have done differently. Then, think about a time when you acted in a way that things turned out well and how you could use those skills in the future. Jot down some notes about what worked and what didn't. Compare the two and notice all the ways the approaches differed. Here's how it will work: Every time you're in a tough situation, and you're about to react and maybe even explode, you're going to use Stop, Think, and Respond and use these notes to help you choose a more productive path.

Okay, so let's get into this! When you're in a situation and want to try what we've been discussing, do the following:

When you STOP, give yourself 1 point. Why 1 point? Because your action was minor compared to the other steps in the big picture. Yet it does deserve recognition, based on the change from your past reactions.

When you THINK about how to approach the situation, give yourself three points.

And give yourself five points when you RESPOND calmly in a sensible manner. When you've completed all three steps, you'll have nine points.

You get the extra point for a total of ten points by reflecting on the incident and deciding if the outcome was better than it could have been otherwise. If the answer is yes, award yourself the extra point and score a perfect ten!

Will you be able to score ten points the first time out? Probably not, but maybe you can score one or four points. Each time you practice, you'll get a little better. Remember: Every point is a little shot of learning by reflecting on what happened this time and how to use Stop, Think, and Respond better next time.

You'll even have a chance to earn partial points. If you're in a situation where you stopped but didn't think, and you went on to your default reactions of the past but later reflected on the event and then did Step 2 (Think), give yourself one point. You get two points if you can see what you could've done differently. Give yourself three points if you returned to the person you reacted to, gave them a sincere apology—with no buts, hidden agendas, or looking for an apology in return. By doing this, you've taken an enormous step forward, and you deserve the full three points because you're building on the new foundation of your life.

Some great resources about sincere apologies include the bestselling book *The Last Lecture* by the late Professor Randy Pausch.[1] A more recent publication, *Why Won't You Apologize?*, a book by Dr. Harriet Lerner, is also a fantastic reference.[2] If you're into podcasts, you can hear Dr. Lerner discuss her book on Brené Brown's podcast series, *Unlocking Us*.[3]

Now that we've gone over the practical application of Stop, Think, and Respond, let's manage expectations. When you master this technique, will you score a perfect ten every time? No! I don't get perfect tens all the time, and I developed this process! No one is perfect every day and in every situation. It's okay, we're human, and we'll have setbacks even when we've mastered this (or any technique). As I said in a previous chapter, did Michael Jordan make every shot he took? No! But he's still considered arguably the best ever to play the game.

The importance of proper communication, thinking about your next step, not taking things personally, and responding instead of reacting is the beginning of the journey to Live Incredibly Full Everyday.

Now you have this new tool in your belt. When the occasion arises, give it a shot. If using this process the first time doesn't go as smoothly as you hoped, don't worry. It's like muscle memory; as you flex your new muscle, it will take some time for your heart and brain to sync up.

Success Activity 5

> Take a look at the Stop, Think, and Respond section of the Activity Workbook. Use the included worksheets to write down interactions you want to review to improve your ability to respond rather than react. Print out as many copies this page as you need to keep working on getting closer to a perfect 10 score!

Time to Celebrate!

You're doing great, I'm so proud of the work you've done! Celebrate your successes and make note of your progress along your journey. Go review these notes occasionally —you'll be shocked by how far you've come!

Chapter 9 —
Words of Encouragement

Congratulations! You've reached the end of Part 2. I'm very excited about the changes you've made and proud of the work you have put into the transformation process. I can't wait for you to experience what's ahead in the following sections of the book!

Part 2 was packed with information. I don't want you to miss out on any techniques that will help you Live Incredibly Full Everyday. If you need to, go back and reread the entire section from start to finish.

Before we move on to the next section, take a moment to look at the changes you see in yourself, even if they're just slight changes. Again, we're not looking for overnight changes or crazy fast transformations.

At this point, you've probably had a few "aha" moments and begun making significant realizations. These realizations may come through reflecting on your past and recognizing one or more of those defining moments, as I did with my brother Michael's death, the 2008 financial crash, and my divorce. Or you might have had an "aha" moment/epiphany like I did when

I was reading *The 4 Agreements* and finally absorbed what it meant not to take anything personally.

People had told me to stop taking things personally all my life, but until that moment, I wasn't ready to hear it. It wasn't until I had begun work on myself that I was open enough to listen to this feedback. Finally absorbing this concept was like being struck by lightning. "Hello, this is why so many of my negative tendencies happen! I'm a control freak, have a short temper, and rationalize pretty much everything—and it's all because I take everything personally!" That one "aha" moment was a game-changer for me.

Even if something like one of these examples hasn't happened for you yet, don't despair. This journey of self-reflection, self-realization, and self-awareness is not a sprint. True transformation takes time. It did for me. Don't worry; these changes will happen for you, too! Remember that these changes happen slowly—instantaneous changes, like yo-yo dieting, don't stick!

One day you're going to look back and say, "Who was that person I used to be? I can't believe I was like that!" Those were my actual words to my wife Sarita when I was telling her a story about my old self Martin 1.0. She looked at me bewildered and said, "I've never even seen a hint of that guy in the few years I've known you."

That was all the validation I needed to let me know that I was now Martin 2.0! The old me needed recognition for everything. This new me was just happy at that moment to have recognized the transformation I had made in myself.

Can you see the possibility of you getting to that point now that you've seen the changes that have just occurred for you in the first chapters? I'm sure there's been a few times when there's been a glimmer of hope as you've read through Parts 1 and 2 and completed the exercises. Remember what I said earlier, don't dismiss that glimmer as a coincidence; it's the magic within you starting to work.

PART 3: REFLECTION FOR CHANGE

"We do not learn from experience… we learn from reflecting on experience."

John Dewey

Chapter 10 —
Reflection Sequence Overview

Welcome to Section 3! I'm so happy for you! Getting through the first two sections shows that you're committed to transforming yourself so you can be a better you, enjoy L.I.F.E., and Live Incredibly Full Everyday!

The first half of this book laid the foundation for what we will delve into here in Section 3. There was a lot of groundwork in Sections 1 and 2, but this section is when the real work begins. The rest of this book will ask you to dig deeper within yourself, so you can create a sustainable transformation and shift your mindset to UNCOVER your greatness!

In the first two sections, we discussed Admission, Cleansing, and Celebration; The Cycle of A's - Ask, Act, and Attitude; and Stop, Think, and Respond. Continue using these methods to transform yourself and shift your mindset. Remember, we're not looking for you to perfect these techniques or even get them right immediately. They're tools to start implementing in your L.I.F.E. as needed when the occasions arise.

Think of the concepts we've already covered as emergency first-aid. They are helpful in emergencies, but you need more powerful tools to address the underlying condition. That's where the concepts in the rest of this book come into play. Think of the first sections as the E.R. tech who saves you from immediate death from a heart attack; the last sections are the cardiovascular surgeon who removes the blockages from your heart.

In the following two sections, we'll examine in detail the acronym UNCOVER. Each letter is a step in my 7-step system to UNCOVER your greatness so you can live your true potential!

Here's a quick rundown of the 7-steps:

U Step 1: Unlock and Unleash
Unlock what's keeping you stuck and Unleash the frustration you're holding on to so you can start your journey.

N Step 2: Navigate
Navigate how to get off your emotional roller-coaster and find what is holding you back.

C Step 3: Choose
Choose the values that are most important in your life.

O Step 4: Obtain
Obtain the tools you need to respond calmly to all situations.

V Step 5: Visualize
Visualize who you want to be from here on out.

E Step 6: Embrace & Enjoy
Embrace the new life you're creating and Enjoy your endless potential.

R Step 7: Reclaim
Reclaim your strong, confident & happy L.I.F.E. to Live Incredibly Full Everyday.

We'll begin by exploring the first three steps: Unlock & Unleash, Navigate, and Choose. As you can see, the first letter U has two parts, Uncover and Unleash, so that we can cover these essential steps in detail. We'll discuss the importance of Uncovering what's keeping you stuck and then Unleashing the frustration you're holding on to.

Before we get into the next chapters, let's discuss why it's essential to reflect on the past so you can create lasting change. As we discussed earlier, you can't change the past, but you can learn from the past to make adjustments in the present. I want to be clear we're not talking about wallowing in the past and throwing a pity party; we're talking about looking at those defining moments that defined who you are now and the actions and reactions you display as a result of those moments.

Ralph Waldo Emerson said, "The mind, once stretched by a new idea, never returns to its original dimensions." That's the idea here. By now, you've identified your trigger point tendencies and admitted they're holding you back. You can't in good conscience go back to who you were before. So, where do you go from here? Now is the time to change those harmful tendencies to healthy ones and move forward boldly. That's why you bought this book, so play full out and go for the gold!

"Getting stuck in the past is like guarding a cemetery."

Hugo Pratt

Chapter 11 — Unlock

Welcome to Step 1 of the UNCOVER approach! The first step —the "U"—stands for "Unlock" and "Unleash."

Step 1 is the most crucial step because if you allow yourself to stay "locked" in the past, uncovering your greatness can never truly begin. This step is so essential that it's broken down into two chapters. This chapter covers how to Unlock what's keeping you stuck, and the next chapter, Chapter 12, covers how to Unleash the frustration you're holding on to.

Let's get started with Unlock so you can begin Living Incredibly Full Everyday! To begin this process, you'll examine any secrets, stories, or shame triggers keeping you stuck.

What I mean by stuck is you can't move forward because you have emotions holding you back from the happiness you deserve. Think about where you are now in your life. Are you happy in your current place in life? What does it look like for you to experience true happiness? Does it come with a price? Maybe that price is feelings of discontent, uncertainty, and disillusionment.

The journey begins by understanding what's keeping you stuck where you are. Put bluntly; you don't know what you don't know. What this means is sometimes you're so emotionally tied to certain feelings (like the ones mentioned above) that you don't understand it's those very feelings that keep you stuck. In these situations, denying when others point out the thing keeping you stuck can be easier than facing the unknown future that healing brings.

Your family and friends may have tried to bring your attention to what's keeping you stuck. Before now, perhaps you refused to admit they might be right. Now is the opportunity to reflect on those conversations and determine if they were trying to help you see the chains holding you back. Reflecting on these conversations can sometimes provide the hidden key to help you identify the core issue to UNLOCK the chains and finally begin to move forward.

Taking this kind of feedback from friends and family can be difficult. If you need to, find a coach or therapist to help you through this process. Let's take an example situation to explore why this can be difficult. Say you're recently divorced and constantly encountering triggers that send you into thought loops about how miserable she's made your life, how walking around an empty home is disheartening, or how eating alone is depressing. Perhaps your family and friends are walking on eggshells around you, afraid to say her name because you might blow up and throw the toaster at the wall. In emotionally charged situations like these, I've found that my clients are much more open to discussing their feelings with someone like me rather than with their family and friends. The reason is that when speaking to a family member or friend, there can seem to be a certain amount of judgment attached to what the friend or family member is saying.

If you find yourself hearing constructive feedback you would prefer to ignore from those close to you, it doesn't matter whether it's true that they are judging you; the fact that you suspect it to be true is enough to close off any forward progress. This is why talking to someone who isn't directly involved can be helpful. Speaking with someone who has no emotional attachment, you can feel there is no judgment—just a supportive ear. This person can hear what you are saying without you feeling that you're being judged, so you can be more open and willing to discuss your emotions.

I know this was true for me when I started to put my life back together while going through my divorce. My close family members would give me advice with all good intentions, but amid the emotional whirlwind at the time, all I perceived was them judging me for getting a divorce. My inner voice constantly told me, "They don't know how it feels! They're not going through it!" Because of this belief, my breakthrough didn't start until I was training to become a life coach. We were paired with other students to trade coaching practice as part of the curriculum. I coached one student in my class, and another student coached me. Having that opportunity to be coached by a completely objective person with no agenda helped open my mind to change. Looking back, it was another of those defining moments that helped me grow into understanding how to Live Incredibly Full Everyday.

I'm a firm believer that you never stop learning. There is always something new to learn, and there's always room for personal growth. I like to keep pressing forward and learning by reminding myself of this quote by Vernon Howard: "Always walk through life as if you have something new to learn and you will." This process starts with understanding that there are emotional blocks, or what I refer to as energy blocks keeping you stuck.

There are some terms I will be using that need to be clarified. Rather than saying emotions or feelings, I prefer to call them energy. Emotions and feelings have too many negative connotations. We all have definitions for them, but there is no good or bad; that's why I call them energy. Energy is how you show up every day. Usually, when you walk into a room, the people around you can tell what kind of energy you're exuding.

The kinds of energy you have will determine your state and may even affect those close to you. If you're unhappy, those around you will feel that low energy and you may bring them down. On the other hand, showing a positive, happy kind of energy may also reflect on others. One of the goals of this book is to help you consciously shift the energy you're putting out to reflect in how you show up in your life.

There is also "hidden energy." This type of energy doesn't serve you or the people around you. An example of this is plastering on a happy face to hide depression. Those around you will still feel this—identifying the energy source will just be more difficult.

Imagine a day when you don't have a care in the world—where everything around you is not happening to you; it's just happening in the normal course of events. You can shift your energy to suit the situation and never feel "stuck" in one energy; you can experience a full range of experiences without being overpowered by them. This process Unlocks your ability to live life vibrantly and with incredible depth. As I said before, this shift is a slow transformation, and with effort can be achieved. It may not seem possible right now, but it is as long as you accept the change.

Energy can neither be created nor destroyed. It is the universal vibration that keeps us all connected. All things, even living and non-living, exist because of the resonance of energy. The higher frequency we resonate at, the more connected we are to our inner health. Your inner health can be defined simply by when your heart and mind are in sync; your inner health is at its greatest when this happens.

Energy Blocks

Now, let's look at energy blocks. Energy blocks prevent you from shifting your energy effortlessly according to the situation. They typically show themselves in anger, frustration, and distrust. These energies inhibit the easy flow of energy and keep you from expressing your powerful, creative abilities, preventing you from living the life you're meant to live. They hold you back, slow you down, and limit your ability to gain success. Relating that to uncovering your greatness, energy blocks can keep you from putting the past behind you and exploring the possibilities of creating the happy life you desire.

So how do you identify these blocks holding you back so you can make a change?

Let's start by identifying five types of energy blocks. In these five blocks, you will find what is keeping you from moving forward and achieving what you want.

It starts with outer blocks; these are outside of you and perhaps out of your control. Economic conditions are an example of outer blocks. For example, the national economic climate affects everything that happens and, for the most part, is out of your control. It's up to you to recognize the conditions and figure out how to work within them. To return to our example of divorce, once the amount of alimony is set, it's up to you to understand how to work within that set parameter to live your own life.

Then there are inner blocks. Inner blocks are those things produced within you. They disrupt and distract you from your success. They can be beliefs you have about your world and your environment, ways in which you apply and integrate your past experiences into the present moment, interpretations you create about events and people, and that inner critic that derails your attempts to achieve and accomplish your goals. By looking at these inner blocks carefully and objectively, you can release their hold on you and the negative, destructive energy attached to them.

Four Types of Inner Blocks

1. Limiting Beliefs are things you accept about your life, yourself, your world, or the people in it that limit you somehow. For example, you may tell yourself, "I come from a poor family; therefore, I can never be rich."

2. Assumptions are expectations that, because something has happened in the past, it will happen again in the future. For example, you may think that having a previous divorce means you will never be able to have a happy marriage.

3. Interpretations are opinions or judgments you create about an event, situation, person, or experience.

4. Gremlins are the inner critics telling you constantly that you're not good enough.

I'll repeat these quotes because they are powerful reminders:
"We do not see the world as it is. We see it as we are."

"The world is what you think it is."

These powerful quotes from the Talmud and Genevieve Davis, respectively, mean wherever you are in your life at any specific moment is how you'll view the world. If you consider your life wonderful and full of adventure and joy, you'll likely see the world as beautiful and abundant. If you see your life as full of hardship and unlikely to change, you may view the world as dark and dreary.

My perception of how and why I got divorced is my version. If you asked my former wife, her perception would be different. Each perspective is valid, but I am responsible for my perception, just as you are responsible for your perception in any situation you experience. Growth depends on the willingness to be open to the probability that your perspective will change over time and your desire to continue improving yourself as you move forward.

You have a lot of emotions tied to your past and many of the outcomes as a result of actions taken. Besides your perspective, your inner critics may also be holding you back. As I said before,

I call these inner critics Gremlins. The Gremlins whisper, "You don't deserve to be happy; you're not good enough." These whispers do everything they can to hold you back and keep you stuck, unable to shift your energy easily.

Imagine if you could flip the script on those Gremlins that constantly reinforce these negative thoughts so instead they reinforce positive thoughts such as, "You have self-worth. You're worth it. You're a wonderful human being. You are good enough. You can do anything and be anything you want." These types of thoughts encourage you to uncover your greatness and find the happiness and success you've been yearning for.

These thoughts will also give you the hope to try again because you will no longer be tied to the idea that what has been will always be. You'll be able to step forward and try again with the understanding that a new outcome is possible.

That's what the Unlock stage is about: figuring out what's happening now, what happened in the past, how to stay in the present, and how to move toward the future. That is when release comes into the picture—releasing the past so you can step into the future.

So how do you unlock the secrets keeping you stuck? It takes the will and desire to look deep inside yourself, admit your weaknesses, and identify your strengths. You're not looking to completely tear yourself down and begin again, but you are searching for those things in your character and your attitude that need tweaking. If you're willing to do the work necessary, the benefits will reward you for the rest of your life.

Now that you know how to identify what is holding you back, let's move on to some practical exercises. Start by examining what your attitude broadcasts to others. Are you so unhappy with your life that it affects everything around you? Is your work suffering? Is your relationship with your family declining? How about your friends? Are they happy to see you, or do they seem distant when you talk to them?

Here's where Unlock really starts. You have to admit that maybe you're the one who is different, not them. Once you accept your attitudes, you can begin letting go of those attitudes and character traits hurting you and everyone around you. Then you can start to forge a new outlook and personality or go back to the way you approached life when you were happiest—use the techniques that serve you well and that serve those you care most about in your life.

L.I.F.E. Assessment

I use a tool with my clients in my coaching practice called the L.I.F.E. Assessment. This online assessment has been beneficial to my clients in evaluating where they are in their lives and where they could make some changes to improve their outlook. After they take the assessment, we review the results together. I interpret the results and identify some of the emotions holding them back. Some areas we evaluate are: How engaged you are in your roles in life, work, and, particularly, your tasks. You learn how you lead—which is the ability to motivate others and yourself to achieve greatness. You also learn about your energy level, level of consciousness, and something called your L.I.F.E. Factor—the higher this indicator is, the better your chances of creating a new mindset and the more successful you will be.

The assessment measures the seven levels of energy in your life. The seven levels, from lowest energy level to highest, are victim, conflict, responsibility, concern, reconciliation, synthesis, and non-judgmental.

The lower your overall score or your Average Resonating Level (ARL) is, the less you have uncovered from the emotional pains of your past. The greater your desire to Unlock and willingness to release the frustrating things keeping you stuck, the sooner your Uncover changes will happen. We then use these results to create a plan of action to help you Unlock with as little pain as possible.

As an example of how these results can help you, I was in the middle of my divorce process when I first took the assessment. My conflict score was 29 percent of my total score, the highest percentage on my scale of seven levels. It meant that my anger level was usually heightened, especially when in a stressful situation, and I was always primed and ready for conflict. About a year and a half later, when I retook the assessment, it was only 9 percent, one of the lowest percentage levels on my scale; the other 20 percent was dispersed among the higher energy levels. It's easy now for me to see the difference in my everyday attitude. My children often comment on how they can't believe the difference in me.

If you're stuck in the Unlock process and are interested in learning more about the L.I.F.E. Assessment, scan the QR on the next page.

Scan for More Information About the L.I.F.E. Assessment

In the next chapter, we'll discuss how to Unleash the frustration you're holding on to, so you can accelerate your transformation journey!

Success Activity 6

> Take a look at the "U" Part 1 - Unlock section of the Activity Workbook. Be completely honest with yourself about what your blocks are (remember—no Rational Lies), and give some examples of how they're not serving you. It's ok to be tough on yourself right now and get out of your comfort zone.

TIP!

Taking a long, hard look at what needs to change is essential to Unlock those feelings and tendencies holding you back so you can Unleash growth!

Chapter 12 — Unleash

Welcome to Step 2 of the letter "U" - UNLEASH the frustration you're holding on to.

In this chapter, we'll discuss the importance of unleashing what is keeping you stuck. Often, what's keeping you stuck are those things in your past that bother or upset you. You might even resent or regret those past experiences. The more you hold onto them, the more you won't be able to move forward and create that new L.I.F.E. you want. Often, there's nothing you can do about the past outcome. By living in the past, you're not allowing the future you deserve to happen.

I like to share quotes about the past with my clients to encourage them through this healing phase. One of my favorites is, "It's not the same thing to know your past as it is to carry the past." Keep this in mind as you move through the Unleash step.

To begin releasing the past, let's start with a simple exercise you can do whenever you want to blow off steam.

Years ago, while working with a client we'll call Ruby; I found that as much as she tried to move forward, she still felt incredible frustration toward her ex-boyfriend. Part of her believed there was a possibility of getting back together with him in a few years. As a result, Ruby continued to carry the baggage of frustration and anger with her because he kept disappointing her by not making the changes she hoped for him to make. Ruby needed to reach the point where she acknowledged her frustration, released her feelings about him and moved forward with her life.

I asked Ruby what she would like to say and do if he was standing in front of her. She said she wanted to punch him in the face! Since Ruby's initial response was unrealistic (and illegal), I gave her an alternative exercise to complete and asked her to report back with her results in our next session. I suggested an activity I created called Snake in the Grass.

I coached Ruby to find a confidant, someone she felt comfortable with, preferably someone very familiar with her relationship with her ex. Then I told her to get an object like a pillow or beanbag chair. With her friend watching, Ruby would then say to the pillow everything she wanted to tell her ex. If she felt so angry that she wanted to hit him at any point, she should hit the pillow. The friend was a witness who could acknowledge and validate Ruby's words.

While expressing frustrations is important, the key point of this activity comes after the first wave of frustration has been expressed. I told Ruby that after the first wave, she should turn to her witness and ask if they thought she had expressed everything she needed to. If the witness thought there was more to be said, Ruby should continue to do this until she felt she got as much as she could out of the exercise. I recommended that Ruby allot at least an hour to ensure she had plenty of time to express everything she needed.

Ruby came to the next session totally exhilarated! She reported that, instead of using a pillow, she took her friend and went into the forest. While in the woods, Ruby found a dead snake (hence the name "Snake in the Grass"). She took a stick and beat the heck out of the snake while yelling at it all the things she wanted to say and do to her ex. When Ruby felt done, she asked her friend if they thought she was holding anything back. After getting their feedback on a few things, Ruby continued the exercise until she felt sufficiently satisfied.

Ruby's ability to release her frustration on the snake allowed her to accept that the relationship was over and put the past behind her. I'm happy to report that her progress after that was fantastic! I recommend this activity to nearly all my clients to clear blockages related to relationships, life experiences, or frustrations they are experiencing that are holding them back from the healing they need.

I believe it's ok to look back to reflect. Not to get stuck in what happened, but so you can understand what got you here and why. As I've said before, there were times in my life that were defining moments. For years I allowed these moments to define me as a people pleaser. I was always on edge because I took everything personally. I was a control freak.

My life was forever changed when I finally understood how my defining moments shaped who I was. Talk about a major "Aha!" moment. Once I identified these turning points in my life, I could finally focus on Unlocking all the chains I had created for myself and finally step forward to Unleash the shame, resentment, and frustration I had been carrying for decades. Now it's up to you to decide where you go from here. Why not make your future the best it can be?

Let's talk about self-awareness vs. self-conscious to help you dig even more deeply into the Unleash process. There's a huge difference between the two phrases. This difference can be crucial in understanding how to avoid subconsciously weighing yourself down with chains again after you progress through the Unlock and Unleash steps.

Self-consciousness is directed from the outside world to your inner self and comes from a place of low-frequency energy—guilt, conflict, and doubt. Self-consciousness comes from a mindset of lack, complaining, and blaming. It involves being concerned with what others think of you and how the situation will affect you and is primarily based in a fear response. For example, when operating from a self-conscious perspective, you probably react to uncomfortable situations instead of responding. When you're self-conscious, you question your decisions. You second-guess yourself and allow other people's opinions and judgments to sway your judgment.

Conversely, self-awareness is more inward-facing and comes from a place of high-frequency energy—acceptance, contentment, and self-assuredness. Self-awareness involves having an accurate and realistic understanding of how you respond to situations and how you feel about things. It enables you to approach interaction and circumstances from a more balanced, richer stance. Self-awareness comes from a mindset of abundance, taking responsibility, and gratitude. Sound familiar?

Being self-aware doesn't mean you don't get angry. Let me clear up a misconception right now; throughout this book, you might think I'm advocating that you should never get angry. Nope! What I'm saying is there are different ways to get angry. Reacting like a Nuclear Reactor is the worst way! Rather than exploding when you get mad, it should be manageable anger. Rather than rage controlling you, experience anger without giving it the reigns to control you and your life.

Here's an example from my own life. About a year after my divorce, my son was getting married. A few days before the wedding, something happened that, in the past, would have resulted in me calling my ex-wife, exploding, and ripping into her. Due to the growth and healing I had been working through, I stopped and thought before I reacted. As I thought about it, I said to myself, "Why upset during the upcoming wedding? I'll wait till afterward to address this issue."

I waited until a few days after the wedding, then called my ex and calmly explained I was upset, and at the end of the call, I finished by saying, "Thank you for divorcing me." It was a moment of closure for me. At that moment, I understood why getting divorced was the best thing to happen to me. I was a new person with a new outlook on LIFE, and my ex was no longer part of that outlook. More importantly, I was very proud of how I handled the situation. I got angry without getting upset and without blowing up like a Nuclear Reactor. My journey into Martin 2.0 was progressing nicely.

There will be times that you're going to be angry. It's a natural feeling that should not be suppressed—just redirected from reactionary to responsive.

For your Success Activity, do the Snake in the Grass exercise for yourself. Remember: this exercise is about finally expressing what you have been suppressing. Be sure to get to the bottom of the issue until nothing is left to express! And a reminder: use a pillow or go out into the forest. DO NOT approach anyone you feel frustrated or angry with. The point is NOT to have a restraining order filed against you.

Once you've successfully completed the Snake in the Grass exercise, move on to the next chapter: Navigate. This chapter will help you step into moving forward with your life.

Success Activity 7

> Grab a pillow and a friend. The pillow is what you're going to focus on while you cry, yell, get physical – whatever YOU need to in order to Unleash the frustration you've been holding on to.
>
> When you feel you've expressed everything, as your friend for feedback. If they tell you to dig deeper, do it! Continue until everything has been fully expressed.

TIP!

The Snake in the Grass Activity is simple, but that doesn't mean it's easy! Be sure to dig deep and express everything you need to!

Chapter 13 — Navigate

Congratulations! You made it through the first part of the UNCOVER process! The first few steps of introducing healing and change are the most difficult. Now that you've taken that step, we'll move on to strategizing these changes and developing the tools to keep progressing forward to the L.I.F.E. you want.

With that in mind, let's move to the second step in the 7-step system to UNCOVER your greatness so you can live your true potential, enjoy L.I.F.E. and Live Incredibly Full Everyday! The "N" stands for Navigate. This step will help you Navigate your emotional roller coaster and understand how it's holding you back.

Oscar Wilde wrote: "A man who is master of himself can end a sorrow as easily as he can invent a pleasure. I don't want to be at the mercy of my emotions. I want to use them, to enjoy them, and to dominate them."

In 12-step programs, participants recite the Serenity Prayer: "God, grant me the serenity to accept the things I cannot change, the courage to change the things I can, and the wisdom to know the difference."

A huge part of moving forward is learning to manage your emotions. It starts by understanding and accepting that you can't change things or people; you can only change yourself. Understanding this is important. While there is a groundswell beginning that advocates for a healthy balance in relationships, it's still common for individuals starting a relationship to believe they can influence their partner to change any habits or traits they find objectionable. Nothing can be further from the truth. My advice for you going forward: If there are things you don't like about a person you may be in a relationship with, don't expect that you can change the person; you're better off ending that relationship.

You may not be able to change others, but you can change yourself. One factor many people find themselves stuck in and have difficulty changing is the emotional rollercoaster I mentioned earlier. You may be stuck on this rollercoaster without realizing it if you are experiencing intense feelings of anxiety, denial, fear, or depression followed by relief, excitement, optimism, or hope. This constant back-and-forth swing is what it feels like being on the emotional roller coaster. Navigate aims to help you turn your emotional roller coaster into a much smoother, more consistent ride.

For myself, when I accepted that I had become a Nuclear Reactor, I realized that my emotions were keeping me from moving forward. I decided to devise a way to understand my emotions when they were happening and figure out how to control my emotions instead of my emotions controlling me. After figuring out this process, I manifested my dreams. You have the power to do this, too! You hold in your hands the result of what I have been able to create after making this realization and developing the tools to stay off the emotional rollercoaster. It is my deep desire that tools help you to do the same.

Now get ready because I'm going to introduce you to another acronym to help you get off your emotional rollercoaster. (I told you I love acronyms!) To make the tool easy to remember in tense situations, it also uses the acronym L.I.F.E. to help you remember the steps. Before I reveal this new acronym, let's discuss why it's important.

As I've said in an earlier chapter, your thoughts lead to your emotions and feelings, which then lead to your actions. In short, something comes into your head, you start thinking about it, and then your feelings and your emotions take over. Then, you often start doing things because of how you feel. You may act on these emotions only to look back later and say, "Why did I do that?!" That's precisely why I want to help you build your emotional strength, so you can navigate your emotional rollercoaster and control your emotions instead of your emotions controlling you.

I've said this in a previous chapter, but I want to make sure you understand. To be clear: I'm not saying you shouldn't have feelings or emotions, just the opposite! I'm saying: Don't dismiss them, bury them, or allow them to overpower you and drive your actions. Figure out how to apply appropriate actions based on what you're feeling. And that's what we'll do here.

Emotions vs Feelings

First, let's answer this question: Is there a difference between emotions and feelings? The simple answer is: Emotions are the underlying energy that can begin in either our conscious or subconscious. Feelings happen when emotions start affecting our bodies and occur in the conscious mind. Generally speaking, feelings are when we begin consciously associating words with how we're feeling.

Now let's go, let's go deeper. An emotion is a physiological experience or a state of awareness brought about by your core self responding (or reacting) to the world you exist in. Once the emotion begins filtering into your conscious mind, it catches your attention, and you begin thinking about it. At this point, it becomes a feeling, more specific, and easier to work through. Eventually, as you become more experienced with this process, you can delve into working with emotions when they occur in the subconscious rather than waiting for the feeling to form in the conscious. Years ago, I didn't understand why the distinction was such a big deal until I started going through my divorce and began understanding the differences between the two.

During that time, there wasn't a lot of separation between experiencing an emotion and the feelings hitting me. I would feel an emotion without acknowledging it (while simultaneously getting overwhelmed without knowing why) and move on. I never slowed down to actually feel. I was careening through life, reacting to my internal state rather than experiencing and exploring it. Similarly, many people are unaware of the emotions they're experiencing. For these people, emotion and consciousness of it are not strongly connected.

Like me, many people don't even realize they're fearful, angry, or depressed. Their emotional state has become so persistent that it drags them into severe moods—moods sometimes so extreme that others begin to notice. You may have experienced this yourself. Perhaps you didn't realize it until somebody pointed out that you had been intensely sad about something in your life. Perhaps you were worried about money, or maybe you were upset about something that happened at work. In not recognizing or being able to identify what was happening inside, you experienced a disconnect between emotions and feelings.

Many people experience this disconnect. The emotions are certainly there. Often, there is no consciousness of emotions at all. They have emotions, but they don't recognize or understand them. And their behavior displays their emotions to others, but the person can't acknowledge or identify what they're experiencing.

This disconnect between emotions and feelings stems from the constant repetitive and relentlessly anti-emotional training we get that tells us emotions are the opposite of rationality (definitely not true), the opposite of spirituality (nope), and the center of the world's problems (not right but wrong-ish).

People are unaware of their emotions because they've been trained since birth to repress, suppress, ignore, demonize, and avoid them. Or they swing to the opposite pole and allow their emotions to explode as soon as they arise. That was me when I was a Nuclear Reactor! I didn't just react; I exploded, leaving trauma and damage in my wake.

The anti-emotional training we all learned isn't helping anybody. It makes us emotionally unaware and emotionally chaotic because an unfilled emotion can bounce around inside us, like a hyperactive pinball. Luckily, if you feel your emotions, you can become more aware and intelligent about your expression of and response to them. That's where the concept of self-awareness vs. self-consciousness we discussed in the last chapter, comes in. Contrary to the repressive training we've all gotten about emotions and feelings, knowing your emotions can actually help you work with them.

Before we get into the four-step process to build your emotional strength, let's begin with a question: How much should how you feel impact what you do? We don't need to look much further than the 11 o'clock news to see the consequences of unchecked feelings. The outside world is just a reflection of what happens so often inside each one of us.

When I began my emotional strength journey, my emotions got the better of me, controlled me, and ultimately led to my divorce. I needed to figure this process out, too.

Digging Deeper Into Emotions and Feelings

So what are we to do with our feelings? Ignoring them or serving them are not good options. Both extremes lead to lost momentum, unnecessary harm, and confusion. How do we feel our feelings without letting them rule and wreck our lives? How do we find balance?

Before we move on to the four-step process to map out how you build your emotional strength and take strategic action no matter what you're feeling, let's review some differences between emotions and feelings. Understanding the difference between the two will be essential to moving through the first steps in the emotional strengthening process.

The charts on the next page will show you the slightly different viewpoints both emotions and feelings will bring to your interactions with your inner world and the world around you. These differences may seem subtle, but they profoundly affect how you interact with yourself and the world.

The first chart shows the differences between emotions and feelings in terms of how we interact with our environment. The second chart gives examples of how to identify the difference between emotions and feelings when we experience them.[1]

Emotions and Feelings: Expression

Emotions	Feelings
Emotions begin in the subconscious.	Feelings filter into the conscious mind.
Emotions are more general but can be more challenging to dig into and define for ourselves.	Feelings are specific and are typically easier to identify once the emotion begins them is identified.
Emotions are psychological and physiological responses to your environment.	Feelings are psychological and physiological responses to what you anticipate happening in the future.
Emotions are similar to fight or flight in that they are an immediate response to your environment.	Feelings are similar to eating a healthy diet in that they are more oriented toward long-term outcomes.
Emotions can be intense but are broader.	Feelings are more nuanced and fleeting.

Emotions and Feelings: Experience

Emotions	Feelings
Happy	Delighted
Caring	Passionate
Fearful	Terrified
Angry	Affronted
Depressed	Desolate

L.I.F.E. Mood Lifter Method: Build Your Emotional Strength

Now that you have a clearer understanding of the difference between emotions and feelings, let's get into the four-step process to build your emotional strength using the L.I.F.E. method and keep your emotions from ruling your actions.

L-Listen
I-Identify
F-Find
E-Engage

Let's go through each step of this process together. I want you to have a firm grasp on this process so you can understand how to utilize this four-step L.I.F.E. Method whenever you have something coming up that you want to work through. My goal is for you to Build Your Emotional Strength so you can experience the full range of emotions and emotions without becoming overcome by them!

L-Listen to your inner voice and acknowledge your emotions.
I-Identify your feelings.
F-Find out why. Examine your feelings.
E-Engage in change and take action.

Step 1: Listen. Listen to your inner voice, and acknowledge your emotions.

Detach from the need to act or judge. What do I mean by that? Give yourself permission to feel. When you feel emotions, you may start judging yourself without realizing it. Or you may begin acting out (or reacting) because you are experiencing fear or anger and deflect these feelings by judging the people around you. When overwhelmed, it's easy to react rather than respond and think about what's really going on. It's okay to have emotions. I'm not telling you not to experience them. I'm telling you to listen to what's going on in your inner voice. Give yourself permission to feel through your emotions and detach from the need to judge or act right away.

Step 2: Identify your feelings. Ask yourself, "What are my emotions? How do I best describe my feelings?"

Refer to the Vocabulary of Emotions and Feelings Chart in the Activity Book (downloadable using the QR code on the Table of Contents page) to help you during this process. You'll go down the list and say: is what I'm experiencing strong, medium, or light? Look for the words in the corresponding column that resonate with you and most accurately describe what you're experiencing. Now, you're acknowledging your feelings! Good work! You're saying, "I am okay to feel this; I'm listening to it; I'm acknowledging my feelings."

For example, if you identify that you're experiencing happiness, you need to identify the specific flavor of happiness you're experiencing. If it's medium, determine if it's light-hearted, lively, or buoyant. If it seems strong, identify if it's energetic, exhilarated, or overjoyed.

If you're experiencing fear, take a breath and determine the "weight" of what you're feeling, then narrow in on what flavor of fear you feel. Does it seem strong, medium, or light? What specific word best describes what you're experiencing?

Use this chart to evaluate the emotions and feeling you are experiencing throughout the day. Being able to name and describe your feelings will help you understand and manage them rather than being controlled by them. For my clients who struggle with emotional disconnect, it helps them to have this chart on hand to refer to when identifying emotions.

Use Stop, Think, and Respond to help you keep from denying, shoving aside, or suppressing your feelings. Stop, Think, and Respond will also help you move away from reacting when interacting with others while you identify and work through the emotions you may have been denying and suppressing for a long time. This process can dig up a lot from the subconscious, so pay close attention to how you are feeling and take a moment to focus on breathing or just sitting quietly if you start feeling overwhelmed. You'll become increasingly skilled at identifying moments of overwhelm before they happen and able to take these moments to avoid them as you continue this process!

Be gentle with yourself. You are retraining old habits that go to the core of how you live each day. This process is going to take time and consistency. You can do it. Believe in yourself, and you will see radical changes.

Step 3: Find out why. Question what you're feeling.

For this step, you will cross-examine your feelings and go deeper. To do this, you'll ask yourself, "Why am I feeling this way?" You may find it easy to explain why you're feeling a certain way. Examine if a recent situation or interaction precipitated this feeling. If there is no easy explanation, the feeling may stem from something in the past.

Once you've identified why you feel this way, ask, "Should I be feeling this?" Cross-examining yourself as if you were in a trial. Ask yourself, "Are these feelings helping me or harming me?" Then ask, "How are they helping me? How are they hurting me?" Considering what you are feeling will help you avoid radical swings on the emotional rollercoaster and prevent you from reacting in situations involving other people.

This step is essential to the process of building your emotional strength. You may recognize this step as a deeper expression of Stop from Stop, Think, and Respond. Each of these tools builds on the others in a dynamic system to help you learn to enjoy L.I.F.E. and Live Incredibly Full Everyday!

Step 4: Engage in change and take action.

How do you do this? Review your answers to steps one, two, and three, and determine what to do – Right. Damn. Now! What can you do right damn now to create what you want and change how you feel?

The first step you can take is to use the tools you've learned so far in this book! Make a plan to use Stop, Think, and Respond every day. Use the Cycle of A's to keep moving forward in your growth. Use Post-it notes on the mirror or the fridge to remind yourself to use these tools. Set reminders on your phone throughout the day—whatever you need to do to remind you to break from old patterns and use the new tools you have.

Step four is also about getting into action and setting a goal for yourself. Do this by putting it on a calendar. Say to yourself,

"By this time, I'm going to be out of these feelings or emotions." This process is all about you. No one else will get you out of the way you feel. You are the only one who can do it. You've got to want to make yourself get through this.

Remember, what you are feeling is neither good nor bad. Keep self-judgment out of the process. In my coaching, I like to use the terms anabolic and catabolic to describe emotions and energy rather than using the words "good" or "bad." Anabolic is something that helps build you up, and catabolic is something that destroys you from within. If you are stuck in catabolic feelings, these will do nothing but hurt you inside. The goal is to become competent at changing catabolic feelings into anabolic feelings that build you up.

To demonstrate how to do this, I want to return to a story we discussed in the last chapter about my son's wedding—this time, we'll examine how managing my emotions affected how I handled the situation.

As I discussed in Chapter 12, years ago when my son was getting married, my ex-wife and I were not on good terms. Something happened about a week before the wedding that I became upset with my ex-wife about. The old me would have called her up right then and there and freaked out about what she had done. Doing this could have ruined the wedding for myself, her, my son, and everyone else by introducing a lot of tension right before the wedding. Instead, I reflected and said, "You know what? I'm going to wait until after the wedding."

I waited a few days after the wedding to call and tell her how I felt about what had happened. I was upset and angry, but it was measured anger. It was a measured response to what was going on rather than a fly-off-the-handle reaction. It was a response rather than a reaction. As a result of controlling my emotions, I ended the conversation by genuinely thanking her for divorcing me. Remember, I didn't want to get divorced. I was terrified of getting divorced because I thought I would never be loved again.

The moment I thanked her, I released the things I was holding on to that, realistically, could never have been. At that moment, I realized I had just taken a huge step forward because I told her what I felt in a measured way, at the correct time, without ruining the wedding for everybody, and while allowing myself to feel those feelings that needed to be expressed.

You may be wondering what you can do immediately to create the change you want in how you feel. Do exactly what I did: Schedule it into your calendar. Write it down; this is an excellent way to start taking action.

As a result of managing my emotions and taking action by scheduling my response to my ex-wife, I'm pleased to say that my relationship with my former wife is now fantastic. We speak often and collaborate on raising our children.

Another method you can use to take action is telling yourself a new story about what is happening in your life. Much of the change in my relationship with my ex-wife came from re-evaluating the stories I was telling myself about the relationship. The world is as you see it! If you see it as problematic and negative, that's what it will be for you. But if you see it as opportunities and positive, that's what it will be. You also decide how the world sees you. We'll be discussing these concepts in greater depth in a future chapter. For now, understand that taking steps toward your goal of emotional strength is foundational in creating the change you want to see.

Success Activity 8

Take a look at the "N" - Navigate section of the Activity Workbook.

Think about a past or current situation and go through each step of the L.I.F.E. Mood Lifter Method. When you reach Step 4, decide what you will do Right Damn Now! Set a date and keep to it. Be accountable to yourself. Print out more worksheets as you need them!

"The greatest freedom is the freedom of choice."

Unknown

Chapter 14 — Choose

In other chapters, we've talked about letting go of the past and moving forward. In this chapter, we will look closely at how to understand what you're moving toward.

To begin, let's talk about values. Values are the things that make you tick and that drive you. Values are principles people live by. They are also a product of the experiences you've had. Your family, your religion, and your community all influence your values. Your values drive you, yet those values may not reflect what you truly want out of life.

There may be times when your heart and your head are not aligned, meaning that what you want to do in your heart is not the same thing your head thinks is right—or vice versa. This situation can create a disconnect in your life and your relationships. For example, in romantic relationships, if you aren't communicating and living by your values, you may compromise rather than stand by your values, resulting in neither you nor your partner being happy and eventually resenting each other.

The same applies to non-romantic relationships. Consider if you've worked for a company whose values are radically different from your own. This situation no doubt caused stress and, over time, began to erode you rather than build you up. This environmental factor is why evaluating values and balancing areas of your life, such as intimate relationships and work, becomes incredibly important when uncovering your greatness.

I'm not saying all your values must be entirely in sync with everyone around you. However, imagine if you had explored and acknowledged these values early on. You may have found values that were not negotiable, and you may not have moved forward with an association or relationship in the first place. While learning experiences are great, no one wants to spend years in a relationship they end up having to recover from. Better to build a solid, clearly defined foundation that is mutually beneficial for the parties involved from the beginning.

When I got married, I thought that whatever I didn't like about my wife, I could change as time went on. And I think she believed the same was true for me. I have since learned a crucial lesson: Do not go into any relationship thinking that you can change the person you're entering a relationship with. It's safe to say that in almost every situation, the other people in your life will not change. If you want balanced, healthy relationships in your L.I.F.E., you must accept people as they are and build from there. It's essential to become the person you desire to be and be able to stand by those values, so the foundations of your relationships are solidly rooted in your values.

All of this leads to the understanding that every decision comes with consequences. Your feelings, thoughts, and actions begin with your values and carry through into your decision-making process. As I discussed earlier, the ability to be self-aware will only serve you for the better as you become increasingly able to identify your values and thereby act on them. Creating an environment focused on your success is an essential element in this process.

"Have To" vs. "Want To"

A massive step in your transformation from your former life to the new one you want to create is realizing if you make decisions from a position of passion or fear. Another way of saying that is this: Are you making a decision consciously or not?

Now it's time to combine this with what we discussed in the previous chapter on emotions and feelings with what we've been addressing here regarding values driving actions. The energy of the emotions and feelings behind the values we observe directly affects our overt actions. There are many shades of values, but all these fall into two main types: fear-based and conscious-based.

Values based on fear are the ones that cause you to take action to avoid punishment or lack. These are "have to's." Conscious-based values allow you to take positive action toward goals, enjoyment, and abundance. These are "want to's." Usually, people do what they "have to" to get to the point of doing what they "want to." A typical example of have to is: "I have to work at this job I don't like and make money so that I can eat and live." In contrast, doing a job you love is a "want to."

Now that we have established the difference between have to and want to, let's look at it as it pertains to unlocking your greatness. In the early stage of understanding what's holding you back, you may feel you have no control over the outcome and that you "have to" settle for whatever happens. However, if you look at each situation in the light of "I choose to do this" or "I choose to do that," you'll get through this process more easily. I'm not saying your life will be perfect immediately and that you should be happy with everything that happens; however, choosing to move forward will accelerate how quickly you can step into your greatness and put the past behind you.

The first step in learning to choose is considering what your thoughts, emotions, and feelings look like regularly. How well is holding your grudge about past actions or people serving you? Are you spending your nights sleepless with the thoughts of what your life could have looked like? Are you constantly wondering how you are ever going to survive after this? Imagine if you recognized that some things are not worth fighting about (and slowly killing yourself over) and accepted that your choices now determine your future happiness. In other words, make choices based on your "want to" rather than your "have to."

You will find as you do this that the heaviness begins to leave your daily life, and breathing gets a little easier each day. Does this mean you no longer encounter troubles and everything is rose-colored? No! It does mean that you can better handle difficulties when they happen, and you no longer feel like you are being flung around on an emotional rollercoaster that you have no control over.

Choose Your Values

Now it's time to choose what values are most important to you. Is it religion? Is it leadership? Is it community? Is it honesty, integrity, or humor? Knowing your values will make finding those with similar values easier because you have a clear view of what you are seeking. Surrounding yourself with others of similar values does two things for you: 1. It helps you clarify your values further, getting more specific about what you believe and why you believe it, and 2. Observing those who espouse to believe the same thing enables you to evaluate their behavior and determine if the values you are pursuing are genuinely in line with your core beliefs. Once you figure out your values and what drives you, you will be well on your way to uncovering your greatness!

I've included a chart on the next page that you can review to choose which values serve you best. You can use them to define who you are now, who you want to be, and who you want the world to see you as.

"I Can't" vs. "I Choose Not To"

When you are going to make any decision, take a moment and ask yourself, "How well does this decision align with the values I have chosen as the cornerstones of my life?"

Do You Value:

Accomplishment	Abundance	Achievement
Adventure	Altruism	Autonomy
Beauty	Clarity	Commitment
Communication	Community	Connecting to Others
Creativity	Emotional Health	Environment
Excellence	Family	Flexibility
Freedom	Friendship	Fulfillment
Fun	Holistic Health	Honesty
Humor	Integrity	Intimacy
Joy	Leadership	Loyalty
Nature	Openness	Orderliness
Personal Growth	Partnership	Physical Appearance
Power	Privacy	Professionalism
Recognition	Respect	Romance
Security	Self-Care	Self-Expression
Self-Mastery	Self-Realization	Sensuality
Service	Spirituality	Trust
Truth	Vitality	Walking the Talk

Let's look at some factors you can use to determine when you are moving away from your core values. When you notice the word "can't" showing up in your daily vocabulary, stop for a moment and look at the state of your mindset. Is your mindset leaning more toward lack or abundance? The use of the word "can't" usually creeps in when we begin feeling we're victims or that nothing ever goes our way. When this happens, we need to shift our energy to feelings of empowerment and understand that our life is in our control.

When we use the word can't, we're really saying that we choose not to do anything about our situation. With the tools you've learned so far in this book, you have the power to ditch the word "can't!" Toss it to the curb! Use The Cycle of A's to re-orient. Follow this with the L.I.F.E. Mood Lifter to take a long hard look at your feelings. Recognize that your actions control your destiny, and you hold the greatest freedom: the power of choice. Use that power to make the changes you want to see in your L.I.F.E.! You have the power to create the L.I.F.E. you want.

Realizing that YOU have power in your life, regardless of how the circumstances of your life appear, empowers you to shift to using "I choose not to." Your overt actions may look the same from the outside, but your inner world will shift radically. For example, someone who says, "I can't exercise because of my health, weight, injury, etc.," is not accepting responsibility for their situation. The person who says, "I choose not to exercise," recognizes that he has the ability but has made a conscious decision not to. The overt actions are the same: exercise isn't happening today for either person, but the empowered individual used his freedom of choice to recognize it's his choice whether or not to exercise.

My goal with this book is to give you the tools you need to move from being someone who feels locked into using "can't" to someone who feels willing and able to use the phrase "I choose not to." You are likely already experiencing changes if you've used the Success Activities as you read this book. If you haven't done any of the activities yet, go back and do them now! These activities help you use what you're learning in this book rather than reading and forgetting it. The goal is for your L.I.F.E. to transform!

Grab a piece of paper and write your three top values, three statements you want to change from "I can't" to "I choose not to," and then three statements from "I have to" to "I choose to."

Success Activity 9

> This Success Activity is simple but not necessarily easy. Take your time considering your responses so change can occur.
>
> In the Activity Workbook, write your three top values, three statements you want to change from "I can't" to "I choose not to," and then three statements from "I have to" to "I choose to." After you finish, complete the Values Assessment, then come back and dig deeper—write down anything that comes up.

Congratulations! You're at the end of Part 3! You have good reason to celebrate. By reading this far, you've entered a journey many people never set foot on. I'm so proud of the work you've done. It is my prayer that more people will begin to do this work.

My goal is to help every person in the world to UNCOVER their greatness—and I need your help. If you're seeing changes in your L.I.F.E. as a result of reading this book, please tell everyone you know! Let's create a world where every person can enjoy L.I.F.E. and Live Incredibly Full Everyday!

"Dreams don't work unless you take action. The surest way to make your dreams come true is to live them."

Roy T. Bennett

PART 4:
ACTION FOR CHANGE

"Each moment describes who you are, and gives you the opportunity to decide if that's who you want to be."

Bruce D. Schneider

Chapter 15 —
Action Sequence Overview

Welcome to Part 4. In Part 3, we delved deeply into reflection strategies. The reflection steps help you explore how you got to where you are and how to move forward. While reflection is foundational to forward growth, nothing will change if you don't take action. To help you through the next phase of your journey, the chapters in this part of the book will cover step-by-step how to put your reflections into action.

We will be covering the final four steps of the UNCOVER acronym: Obtain, Visualize, Embrace & Enjoy, and Reclaim. The goal of this section is not to give you "quick fixes" that will get you immediate results in one area of your life while harming other parts. Instead, we will focus on sustainable and permanent solutions you will incorporate into your new Living Incredibly Full Everyday lifestyle.

I know what you're thinking: "Come on, Martin! You're not serious! How can you make a claim permanent change will happen?" I can make that claim because I am a walking, talking example of completely changing who I was to who I am now.

As I've written before, I'm now Martin 2.0. Does that mean I'm done growing? No way! I'll never stop learning, and I'll never stop growing. And neither should you!

If I'm coming through as emphatic, good! You've got to do what's necessary to get to what you want to achieve. It's that simple, and it's not that easy. Real change means real work and real sacrifice. The sacrifice I'm talking about is your willingness to sacrifice those unwanted tendencies you've been living with all this time. Remember, I was a people pleaser. I took things personally; I was a control freak. I needed recognition and validation for the things I did to please others. And worst of all, I reacted to everything to the point of overreacting and being a Nuclear Reactor!

Now I can happily say I'm a recovering people pleaser. I don't take too many things personally. I've let go of the need to control things. I'm no longer looking for anyone's approval. And I can confidently say I'm no longer a reactor; I respond to almost all situations. I can also say I have more conversations these days rather than the confrontations that used to dominate my interactions.

I'd like you to re-read that last paragraph and notice there are no absolutes in any of those statements. There's a good reason for that. I want to make this very clear: I'm not perfect. There have been times when I have slipped. Times when I've reacted or tried to please others. When these tendencies pop back up, I'm now aware of doing it, and I can quickly reflect and work on correcting the situation calmly. I know, without a doubt, these tendencies will show up from time to time. My message is: Don't look for perfection; look for good, and then look for great.

Now onto the action steps. These steps will help to reinforce everything you've learned up until now. I've said it before (and I'll say it again): You're on a journey. To make sustainable changes in your L.I.F.E., you've got to be willing to do the work, not complain about it to anyone. Not even to yourself!

I recommend to my clients that they refrain from telling anyone what they're doing as they go through these steps. I'm making the same recommendation to you. Take it from one who knows. No one cares about what you say you're going to do. They only care about what you actually do. That comes by putting into practice the exercises and Success Activities you've learned so far. That means going about your business and not drawing attention to the changes you're experiencing. Wait for people to notice and say something to you. They'll say things like: "You've changed," or "Wow, I wasn't expecting that response!"

Your response to these observations is key. It's very easy to slide back into old behaviors here. You'll want to bust and tell them everything. Take my word for it, don't. Just say, "Thank you." If they persist, say, "I appreciate you noticing," and leave it at that. It will be difficult not to expound. I'm not saying never to tell people. I'm saying to wait until your changes are sustainable.

If you speak too soon and slip, people will think, "I knew it; the change was just a blip." That energy is difficult to overcome when it surrounds you and can undermine your progress. I want you to experience what long-term change with these concepts can be like, so keep quietly making changes until they are hard-wired into your DNA!

When you feel you've made lasting changes, then you can discuss it. You can even tell them about this book and how it's helped you make sustainable changes. Until then, keep going on your L.I.F.E. journey so you can Live Incredibly Full Everyday!

"No one can make you feel inferior without your consent."

Eleanor Roosevelt

Chapter 16 — Obtain

You have now reached the "O" in UNCOVER: Obtain. This step in the process is about obtaining the abundant mindset you have been working toward and stepping into responding consistently rather than reacting. This book has many tools for you to use. This chapter is where you tie these practical tools together in practice.

Let's begin with Stop, Think, and Respond. As discussed in Part 2, how you respond to a situation will determine the outcome. Think before you act. Respond, don't react.

Take a moment and let that sink in more deeply. Think before you act. Respond, don't react. Observing these steps consistently is how you begin to Obtain the results you've been looking for—both in your professional life and your personal relationships.

Let's walk through an example so you know what this can look like in practical terms. I'll give you an example.

In this scenario, Joe wanted to spend more time with his kids after his divorce. He had the kids during weekends while his ex-wife, who we'll call Stephanie, had them during the week. Suddenly, Stephanie decided she wanted the kids during the week-end, too. Joe became distraught and furious. He reacted immediately and got very upset, resulting in a huge fight.

When he and I examined the situation, I told him, "Joe, imagine if you decided to think about it for a moment and respond in a way that was right for you without getting into a fight."

He thought about it, and he said, "You know what? That's very true. I did not think of it. I was just so upset at that moment that I just reacted."

I responded, "Well, one of the things you can do, even in moments of sudden emotion, is to not react. Instead, take that moment to think about what you want to say, then respond. You'll be better off, and the result will be more to your liking."

Joe realized while he had been using Stop, Think, and Respond in his life; he needed to remember to use it when he needed it most: in high-tension situations. He began employing Stop, Think, and Respond even when his emotions and feelings were heightened. Joe watched as his friends and family began responding–rather than reacting–without realizing it!

Over time, you will learn how to control your emotions to best serve you rather than control you. I'm not saying you should never get angry. It is more about deciding what is important to you and making a decision about what response will best serve you.

The first thing you should understand and accept with every kind of relationship is that how you choose to "show up" is entirely in your control. No matter what anyone tries to "do to you," how you react will decide what happens. Try to respond instead of react. You know how to use Stop, Think, and Respond now—so use it! You won't ever regret stopping and taking the time to think before responding.

Five Methods of Dealing With Conflict

Let's revisit the concept we discussed in Chapter 8 about how to deal with conflict. The tools we're discussing will help to decrease the number of conflicts you experience. However, miscommunication and conflicts can still happen, especially when you're beginning to learn how to use these tools.

To help you navigate these high-tension events rather than succumb to them, let's examine methods of dealing with disagreements so you can choose the one that makes the most sense when encountering a developing conflict.

1. Suffer.

You can be a victim. Suffering through is a level one approach framing the situation as "Everything's just going to happen to me anyway, so I'll just say whatever." I don't recommend taking this approach.

2. Accept it.

You could say, "So, what? Does this really affect me?" You can ask yourself if this issue will still matter a year or even a week from now. You may find yourself using this approach as you become more comfortable with the Stop, Think, and Respond sequence.

3. Change the situation.

Do what you can to bring the situation closer to a resolution. Remaining calm can go a long way toward de-escalating conversations. It can also help to approach disagreements with compromise in mind. A good go-to phrase for this is, "I want to find a solution here that we are both comfortable with."

4. Avoid it.

You know what? You don't have to attend every argument you're invited to. It's up to you to decide whether or not you want to fight.

5. Alter the experience.

If you look at it in a different way, the experience will change. It's your world. Choose to create it as you wish.

You decide which method of dealing with conflict you want to use for the situation you are experiencing. Remember: It's your world; choose to create it as you wish—that includes creating change in conflicts!

You Are The Master of Your Thoughts and Decisions

Here are a few quotes I like to keep in mind when conflicts arise.

> "Each moment describes who you are and gives you the opportunity to decide if that's who you want to be."
> *Bruce D. Schneider*

> "No one can make you feel inferior without your consent."
> *Eleanor Roosevelt*

When I first heard "No one can make you feel without your consent" a few years ago, it immediately became one of my favorite quotes. Since then, I have tried to live my life by that quote. It's up to you to decide when someone puts you down how you want to feel about what they said. If you choose to allow it to affect you, it will. However, if you decide to ignore the person's comments and accept that you are the master of your thoughts, you will be able to live a much happier life. Live life on your terms.

> "When you allow what someone says or does to upset you, you're allowing them to control you."
> *Joel Osteen*

It is so important not to take anything personally in your life. It's not an easy thing to do, but it can be a life-changer for you. Not taking things personally keeps you from giving away the power to maintain your values and emotional strength.

Putting experiences and interactions in perspective is easier with strangers and relationships you aren't heavily invested in. You'll find you need to work a lot harder on not taking things personally in your close relationships; this is especially true if you and the other person are used to reacting and taking things personally. Adjustment won't be easy, but it will radically change your relationship.

Here's an example of what I'm talking about: If you were walking down the street, and a total stranger came up to you and told you, "You're an idiot," you'd look at that person, walk away, and say, "I don't really care what that person says. He has nothing to do with me in my life. He doesn't even know me." But imagine if someone close to you came up and said, "You are an idiot." You would react, take it personally and be upset.

Work on shifting your reactions to responses and then to no response—in all your relationships. I know it's easier said than done, but if you give it your full effort, you will start feeling less stressed and more cheerful when you don't take anything personally. Take it from someone who's been there; now that I don't take things personally, I can never feel like someone is trying to hurt me. My life is in my control.

Live Your L.I.F.E.; Don't Try to Live Someone Else's

Remember this quote next time someone says something you usually get upset about: "What you say is about you; what I hear is about me."

Understand that whatever someone tells you is more about what is going on in their life than what is going on in your life; they are just deciding to offload it onto you. It's your decision whether to accept what they're saying and do something about it. Trust me, choosing not to accept it is not easy. It takes a lot of practice, and you won't get it right away, but the more you practice making the decision not to accept others projecting their problems on you, the more you will enjoy the benefits of doing so.

This next quote from Terry Cole-Whittaker may help in situations you find difficult not to react to: "What you think of me is none of my business."

I love this quote. Nothing could have been further from the truth when I started my journey. I wanted to know what everyone and anyone was saying about me and then try to either defend it, dispute it, or live up to it. However, as I proceeded to go through the coaching process, I began to understand that I was living my life with the wrong set of values. They were other people's views of what they wanted me to be like, and I was always trying to please everyone else, generally to my detriment.

I finally learned that the more I tried to please everyone else, the more I failed to satisfy them and the more internally conflicted I became without understanding why. Once I began to understand and accept that my values are mine and mine alone, I began to realize that I only needed to please myself, and as a result, my positive energy would please those around me. I learned that telling people what you were going to or had done was wasting energy, and just living your life to its potential speaks volumes about who you are and what you want.

As you put these tools into practice, you will start to feel like an enormous weight has rolled off your shoulders. A considerable part of your journey involves having your heart and mind on the same page. Simply put, before you start using these strategies, there are times that you do or say things that you don't believe or don't want to believe. As a result, your actions don't make you happy; they actually upset you. When you use the tools mentioned here in your everyday life, your heart and mind will come into alignment.

I'll use my own life as another example of this. In the time leading up to asking for a divorce, my ex-wife kept telling me that I needed to go to therapy. Of course, prideful as I was, I resisted. I told her that it was only her perception. My position changed when my ex-wife said she wanted a separation. The thought that I would ever be divorced was mortifying, and in a panic, I decided I would go for therapy in an effort to save my marriage. This decision didn't save my marriage, but it did radically change the course of my life.

After a few months of going to therapy, I decided to investigate becoming a life coach. I looked at my life and realized I was not serving the principles (values) I believed in. I had always tried to please everyone else: my parents, wife, and family. I had been a businessman my whole life, but my true desire was to help others.

At about the same time I made this life-changing choice, my wife decided she wanted to move forward with a divorce. I could have told myself, "Now that my attempts to save my marriage were unsuccessful, I can forget about moving forward with my thoughts about coaching." But by that time, the work I had done on improving myself had taken root, and my heart and mind were in alignment. I was determined to move forward with plans to become a life coach.

Judging Only Drains Energy

We're all about quotes in this chapter! What can I say? It can help to hear someone else say something encouraging that you know to be true. So here is another great quote for you to think about. This quote is from Wayne Dyer, who wrote, "When you judge another, you do not define them, you define yourself."

A huge part of moving forward is understanding that judging people does you no good. You don't know what has gone on in their lives. It's time to allow everyone else to live as they see fit. Your judgment of their life won't necessarily change anything anyway. Think about the Golden Rule. Not "the one who has the gold makes the rule," but the one that says, "Do unto others as you would have others do unto you." If you don't want to be judged, it has to start with you not judging others.

The beginning is to learn to accept the people around you for who they are. The next part is to decide which people you want in your life. If someone is always negative and judgmental and being around them brings down your energy, you should re-evaluate your relationship. If they are someone who has to be in your life, remember what I talked about earlier: Don't take anything personally. Just let the negative things they say roll off your back and make a conscious decision not to let it affect you. This process won't happen overnight, but with practice and time, it will get easier until they don't upset you anymore.

I like to keep in mind that "Our level of true awareness is directly related to our lack of judging." My definition of judging is forming a negative opinion about someone or something. Living in the physical world means living in duality: light/dark, hot/cold, happy/sad, etc. One side of duality judges things as positive and the other as negative. To be non-judgmental, we must take a quantum leap past duality, away from ego, to a place where we can see other people for who they really are—beautiful and powerful beings experiencing the physical world—and realize we are each on our own journey.

There may be circumstances in your life that you blame yourself or someone else for. It probably became so ingrained in you that it carried over into everything in your life and now may hinder uncovering your greatness. If you can eliminate judgment from your thinking, you'll be able to view everyone and everything in a different light. You'll be able to talk with your family and friends without feeling like your life is under a microscope. This ability will serve you in everything you do and give you more energy to devote to Living Incredibly Full Everyday.

Theory of Reciprocity

I will close this chapter with a look at the "theory of reciprocity." This theory refers to responding to a positive action with another positive action and rewarding kind actions with more kind actions. The theory says that when you interact with people, your interaction is greatly enriched when positive, caring action is chosen. Reciprocity means that people are frequently nicer in response to friendly actions and more cooperative than the self-interest model predicts.

Have you ever taken a day and decided to smile at absolutely everyone you meet—friends and strangers? If you have, you probably know the typical reactions. If you haven't, you should try it. Smile and be nice to everyone you meet tomorrow. You'll be surprised by the reactions; most people you greet with a smile will reciprocate with a smile back. As the day goes on, you'll find yourself conversing with and even laughing with some of your new friends. The feeling you'll get will be wonderful. Think for a minute about the feeling you'll be giving them—one that can be infectious and that they may even pass on or "pay forward" the feeling.

It's a lot like the ocean; it covers so much of the planet, but it's made up of single drops of water. You are a drop of water creating the ocean. By controlling your initial action to be something positive and staying consistent with your efforts, you can eventually affect change, transforming the reaction into a positive response.

If you can refrain from judging those around you, eventually, they may reciprocate by not judging you. Now apply this concept to your bad relationships—without dwelling on the interactions you usually have with them. You'll be surprised by the results. I did with my former wife, and we can now communicate calmly.

Remember the quote by Bruce D. Schneider: "Each moment describes who you are, and gives you the opportunity to decide if that's who you want to be."

There is no such thing as "finally getting it right." This idea traps us into thinking that there are goals to be met at the "end," and we have to perform to meet these goals. We often set goals (to finish school, get married, have a child, earn a Ph.D.). These goals are motivating factors, but to live in the moment, in the present time, means not measuring success in the realization of a goal but by the process. It is in the process that we can decide our measure of success. Life is a journey, a becoming, a growing, a process. Life can be bumpy, but it can also be incredible; remember to fully enjoy your L.I.F.E.!

Success Activity 10

> Look at the "O - Obtain" activity in the Activity Book. Use this technique to help you obtain an abundant mindset by looking at situations from several points of view.
>
> Choose a story you tell yourself regularly, such as, "These things always happen to me. I never catch a break!" Now look at this story from another point of view.

TIP!

Try looking at the stories you tell yourself about the people in your life from a more positive point of view and see what comes up. You may be surprised by some of the conclusions you come to!

Chapter 17 — Visualize

Welcome to the fifth in my 7-step system to UNCOVER your greatness! Are you beginning to enjoy L.I.F.E. and Live Incredibly Full Everyday? This step will cover "V," which stands for Visualize. You will use the tools in this chapter to visualize who you want to be from here on out.

Visualizing is a powerful method of creating an image or representation of what you want the new you to look like, how you want the new you to act, and what you want life to look like for the new you. Having an image you can look at will convince your mind that you can achieve your goal of being the new you. Keep in mind as you move through this chapter that to more specific you make your goals, to more motivated you will be to achieve them, and the more likely it will be that you will reach them.

For example, many people have experienced radical body changes in recent years. If you are like many others right now, you have a fitness goal you want to reach. You could want to work on your health, work on your physical conditioning, or even go back to the size you were when you were younger. A great way to visualize this would be to find an old picture of yourself that represents how you'd like to look again. Without vividly visualizing, you won't be able to know which direction to move.

Designing a vision is exciting, purposeful, and fulfilling. It will inspire you to create whatever it is you want. Ultimately, the vision you see is who you really want to be or what you want to experience. Once you have the image firmly in mind, the vision is activated and set in motion. It's up to you to set the goals you want to achieve. A coach or mentor can be invaluable in helping you set your goals and stay on task.

Did you notice how the process above resembles the Cycle of A's (Ask, Act, Attitude)? You would be right! Ask for what you want (see the image in your mind or put it on paper; visualize), Act to get what you want, and maintain the Attitude to keep moving toward it and receive it when it happens. Remember: It's called a cycle for a reason; you'll continue repeating these actions throughout the journey.

Visualizing (Ask) who you want to be from here on out requires goal setting to develop the image in your head into more than a daydream. Setting actionable goals builds on what you've visualized by sitting down and creating a plan for getting there. By setting goals, you are starting to put into action the ideas you're visualizing (Act).

So why is setting goals so important? You probably spend a lot of time thinking about where you are in your life and where you want to go. In our case, how quickly do you want to UNCOVER your greatness? Goals are essential because they give you something to focus on, making your goals actionable and tangible. If your goals only exist in your head, your chances of success reduce dramatically.

You are well on your way as a Warrior. Continue to set yourself up for success by mapping out your plan for achieving your goals. Write this plan down, read it daily, and put your plan into action. Don't get discouraged if you miss a day. Everyone has setbacks; it's only natural. Just pick up where you left off. As I've discussed before, you're on a journey, and like with most journeys, you take one step at a time.

If you're wondering how to start making a plan, I have some tips for you! The goal-setting strategy I'll share here will help you in a variety of ways. You'll take control of your life. You'll focus on the important things and not get distracted by unnecessary details. You'll make sound decisions without wasting time second-guessing yourself. You'll finish each step toward your goal efficiently. You'll be self-confident and enthusiastic. You'll make progress. You'll be closer to success.

Setting any goal will help you reach your result faster, but I like to be even smarter about setting goals. The technique I use is called AIM SMART goal setting. This method allows you to set goals that help you move closer to your desired outcome and develop an action plan to achieve them. When you set a goal for yourself, you need to AIM toward working on realistic goals.

The AIM SMART Method

Acceptable: What is the acceptable minimum you can do?

Ideal: What is the ideal you want to attain?

Middle: What is in the middle? What's a realistic stretch you're willing to do?

Once you have the goal to AIM for, you follow the SMART process:

Specific: What is the very 1st step of any action/learning/goal identified? Be precise.

Measurable: For what you've listed in Specific, make sure you can measure (qualify or quantify) the success.

Achievable: Is the initial step possible to achieve?

Reasonable: How reasonable is what you're saying you will do? Can it be done at this time?

Time-Oriented: When will you complete this 1st step of the goal (not the entire goal)?

Let's continue with the better health illustration. That's your AIM—get in better physical health and shed some pounds. It's up to you to decide how to go about that. You decide how much weight you want to lose. That's a specific goal. That measurable goal is saying how much. Then you ask, "Is it achievable? Can I lose the weight I want to lose?" Next, ask yourself, "Is it reasonable? Am I setting myself up for failure, or am I setting myself up for success?" Last, make it time-oriented.

Using the weight-loss example, say you decide you need to lose 15 or 20 pounds. If you said to yourself, "I need to lose 15 or 20 pounds, and I need to lose it in two weeks." That's not reasonable. It's not achievable. It's time-oriented, but it's not reasonable. Instead, you need to take a step back, maybe do some research, and come up with a goal that is: specific, measurable, achievable, reasonable, and time-oriented.

As a coach, my job is to be a knowledgeable accountability partner. As an accountability partner, I work with my clients to set different SMART goals during their journeys. Having someone to hold you accountable helps keep you on track to meet your SMART goals. According to the American Society of Training and Development, having an accountability partner increases your chances of success to a 95 percent likelihood of meeting your goals.[1]

In your life, you're accountable to many people: your boss (or clients), significant other, children, friends, and society. Like most people, you've likely felt like you needed to get things done because you had to answer to someone outside of yourself. If you wanted to do something for yourself and were able to be accountable yourself, that's great. Many people need an external source to hold them accountable. When they don't have this source, they say, "Well, it's all right. I'll do it later. I'll do it another time." You don't say that to your boss or clients. Using this excuse repeatedly in your relationships would create huge issues. Why, then, do you do it to yourself?

If you need help staying accountable, that's okay! It doesn't mean you're weak or undetermined. It just means you are very socially minded. If this is the case for you, have a friend or coach as an accountability partner to help you continue toward your goal, even when things happen in your life or your motivation dips.

I'll give you an example of this from my own experience. Lauren was a fellow coaching student with me in coaching school. During a conversation, I let her know I had lost thirty pounds. Our trainers encouraged students to start coaching each other as a way to practice our coaching skills. When Lauren approached me about coaching her on weight loss, I quickly jumped at the chance.

At our first session, we discussed her ideal weight and a realistic time frame to lose weight. I coached her to get very specific on her end goal. She started by visualizing what she would look and feel like when she reached her goal. Given that Lauren was very visual and her goal was to wear a cute swimsuit during the summer, I recommended she cut out photos from magazines of models wearing the same bathing suits she wanted to wear. Placing these photos around her house, like on her refrigerator, served as a constant reminder of what she was working toward.

I asked Lauren to imagine how she felt at her goal weight to dig deeper into her goal. She replied she wanted to exercise consistently and feel like she was living healthily. She didn't just want to lose weight; she wanted to be healthy and create a healthy lifestyle. She was visualizing herself on the beach the following summer in one of the smaller-sized bathing suits on her refrigerator, maybe even a bikini. She was apprehensive about envisioning that, but she decided to stretch herself.

We scheduled to meet once a week for accountability calls. We reviewed Lauren's AIM SMART goals each week and revised them as she progressed. When Lauren started, she was not exercising at all, and, in her words, her diet was "completely unhealthy." Based on Lauren's answers, we decided she would start slowly making changes to sustain her progress over the course of reaching her goal.

During our weekly meetings, Lauren was excited to share her progress. She told me each week that she was motivated by her desire to achieve her goal and not disappoint her health and wellness coach.

From a coaching perspective, I told Lauren she could never disappoint me because I would always be in her corner cheering her on, with no judgment whatsoever. Her answer was that since I was her accountability partner, she wanted to ensure she was staying accountable. There were weeks when she made no or little progress. Usually, during those weeks, she would beat herself up, but together we reset her short-term goals and got her back on track.

For Lauren, being accountable to another person made all the difference in reaching her goal. After six months of coaching, she met those goals! She exercised four days a week for at least one hour each day. Her eating habits completely changed, and she ate healthy most of the time. She reached her goal, lost 50 pounds, and put on a bikini from one of the photos for the first time since she was a teenager. I'm happy to report that she has kept the weight off and continues to eat healthily. She achieved her long-term goals, and she told me maintaining it was easy because of her newfound self-confidence and because she had created her new ways as her new lifestyle.

Success Activity 11

Find "V - Visualize" in the Activity Book. Now it's your turn to start setting some goals.

For this activity, stretch yourself! Remember to set goals that are reasonable and achievable. Have fun with this, and work on setting one goal at a time.

TIP!

It can be easy to get excited about the goal-setting process and set a laundry list of goals you won't keep consistent with. Be aware of this and work on setting one goal at a time for now.

As you become better at accomplishing goals, you can gradually increase the number you are working on simultaneously. Still, I recommend keeping the list between 1-2 major goals at the same time.

"Start by doing what's necessary; then do what's possible; and suddenly you are doing the impossible."

St. Francis of Assisi

Chapter 18 — Embrace & Enjoy

Welcome back to the next step to UNCOVER your greatness so you can enjoy L.I.F.E. and Live Incredibly Full Everyday! Step 6 is "E" for Embrace. You will be embracing the new L.I.F.E. you're creating while enjoying the endless possibilities open to you now.

Are You Engaged?

I don't mean engaged to be married. I mean, are you engaged in what you're doing? Do you take advantage of every moment you have? Do you "seize the moment"? Are you all in when you show up to any situation, any type of encounter, and any kind of conversation? Are you giving your all to the event? Are you one of those people who, when you walk into a room, it's like a light just turned on, bringing your excitement to everyone around you?

Being engaged is a huge part of embracing the new life you're creating. It starts by recognizing that how you show up determines what happens. Remember when we talked about energy in Chapter 11? The level of energy you bring to a situation determines how you show up. I don't mean you have to be super energetic all the time and bouncing off the walls. What I mean is: Are you showing up as your 2.0 self; are you bringing that powerful, confident, centered 2.0 energy?

Karen's Story

Let's look at a client of mine, Karen, who felt like an old, out-of-date, worn-out purse that no one would be interested in after her divorce. The divorce took everything out of her, even though she decided to end the marriage in the first place. Her ex-husband never treated her with respect and always took her for granted. It got to the point she felt like another piece of furniture. Worse, she felt like a piece of furniture that was neglected.

It took every ounce of courage Karen had to ask for a divorce. Her ex-husband told her that he was the best thing that ever happened to her and that she would never find someone to love her. He even went so far as to tell her, "No one will ever love you like I do." She started to believe this gaslighting and almost dropped the divorce, but the little amount of dignity she had convinced her it was time to leave. She finally figured being alone was better than being with someone who didn't respect or care for her.

When she started working with me, Karen looked like she was walking around with a dark cloud over her head. Her self-esteem was so low that she was utterly unengaged. Whenever her friends and family saw her, they were worried and very concerned for her well-being. She couldn't even conceive that she could be happy again. As she opened up about her fears and inner energy blocks, the cloud over her head began to lift. Once she began to reveal the factors that were keeping her stuck and released her frustrations about what her ex had said to her, she became more open and positive. She engaged in uplifting activities, like exercise classes and going out with her friends.

Since Karen had no children with her ex, her interaction with him was limited, so she didn't have to hear his snide remarks regularly. When they did interact, she didn't allow his comments to affect her. Her friends observed a twinkle in her eye and the spring in her step again. She was a new woman looking forward to forging ahead with her new life.

How Are You Adapting to Your Newly UNCOVERed Greatness?

Adapting is simply another word for changing—changing to fit your new life. Adapting is what you've been doing by going through the UNCOVER process! With the right attitude, you can adapt to anything life throws your way.

I know what it means to adapt to a radically new approach to life! From my divorce to losing absolutely all my financial assets and means to become a life coach—my life has been full of radical changes. During each of these changes, I had to adjust my daily living to survive and then learn to thrive. Let me tell you about one of these instances.

I come from a close-knit Orthodox Sephardic Jewish community in Brooklyn, New York. It is traditional in this community (and most observant Jewish communities) to observe the Sabbath every week from sunset on Friday to sunset on Saturday. Dinner on Friday night is always a big deal because this meal opens the celebration of the Sabbath.

Food is a central theme in Jewish households. Over the centuries, family recipes were sometimes the only thing the Jewish people could take as they were forced to move from place to place. These traditional recipes evolved with each new location until there were an incredible number of traditional recipes—many of which are still used today.

Using food to understand and deal with change is something I have experienced in my life, too. During my first marriage, my ex-wife was a fantastic cook. She just had the knack; she was always creating new dishes. When we would tell her the dish was delicious and she should make it again, she'd replied, "I don't remember what I put in it!" We used to joke that if she ever got up the nerve to be a host on a Food Network show, she should call it The Forgetful Chef.

My ex-wife hosting a cooking show wasn't a stretch; she was so good that other families in our community loved being invited to our home for holiday meals. She was also so good that those same families wouldn't ask us to their homes for dinner because they thought they couldn't live up to her reputation. My kids had become accustomed to incredible holiday dinners with their mom in charge of cooking.

After I moved out of the house I had lived in for almost 25 years in New Jersey and back to Brooklyn, there were many things I had to adapt to. Cooking was at the top of the list. I had big shoes to fill. Much to my surprise, I was soon cooking full holiday dinners!

A perfect example was my and the kids' first Thanksgiving. One of my sisters came for dinner, while three others and some of their kids came for dessert. With the assistance of my two sons, who learned to love the art of cooking from their mother, I cooked a full Thanksgiving dinner, including deep-fried turkey, garlic-roasted mashed potatoes, two kinds of salad, yams, and string beans.

With all this cooking, I was feeling fancy and decided to surf the Internet to learn how to roast chestnuts. If you know anything about a Google search, when you start to put in a word, Google tries to interpret what you're searching for. While typing "roasted chestnuts," I also found roasted chestnut soup. I decided, "Hey, why not?" My sister and brother-in-law were stunned by the whole meal,—especially my roasted chestnut soup!—because it was so good.

After making the soup, I had to do something else I never did: cut fruit for dessert. The Internet came to the rescue with videos on how to slice pineapple and melon, and the list went on and on. When the rest of the family came for dessert, they were shocked at the spread we served, including my son's pumpkin pie.

That meal's success revealed a passion for cooking I never knew I had. I've gone from not having a clue how to use a whisk to hosting a weekly Youtube cooking show! By adapting to the circumstances, I was able to express myself more fully while creating wonderful memories with my kids. I would never have discovered this side of myself if I had decided to sit down and give up all those years ago.

Change can be challenging, but it can happen if you're willing to transform. You will have to adapt to your new life as you shed old habits. You can even master tasks you are entirely unfamiliar with right now. (Expert tip: Google and Youtube are fantastic resources for building new skills.)

> "Life offers neither problems nor challenges, only opportunities."
>
> *Unknown*

To call something a "problem" is to create a disempowering judgment. There are no problems, only opportunities for increasing potential on this amazing journey called life. If you take every situation as an opportunity, you will begin to believe that anything is possible. It's like the old saying, "It's not what happens to you; it's how you react"—or, as I like to say, respond. Whatever happens in your life, try to find a way to look for the opportunities that can result from the situation. With uncovering your greatness, look at it as an opportunity to start over and learn from the past so you can create a new life. See that in your new life, anything is possible; you are the only one setting the limits.

Forgiveness

When I decided to write my first book, *Recovering From Divorce*, I was considering whether I would write about forgiveness.[1] I was thinking about not including it because it is difficult for many people to let go of the past. They're holding on to so much resentment, anger, and mistrust. The last thing they want to consider is forgiving others who hurt them. They might even want to kill them if they thought they could get away with it.

Even suggesting forgiving those people is often out of the question for someone just starting to uncover their greatness. However, as uncovering progresses and you're to the point of creating your new life, you may begin to accept the idea of forgiveness. I'm not talking about actually seeking out that person and telling them you forgive them, especially since they'll probably look at you like you're crazy. To complicate matters further, many people you think of when forgiveness comes up may not even recognize that they did anything requiring forgiveness.

Harriet Nelson so eloquently stated the concept of forgiveness: "Forgive all who have offended you, not for them, but for yourself." As you've gone through the steps of UNCOVERing, you've probably begun to recognize that this process is about becoming a better, new you. Included in that new you, you're letting go of the past and focusing on today and tomorrow. It's all about finding peace within you.

At this point, the amount of time you experience anger and resentment has likely begun to reduce. As it reduces, the need to think about how you were disrespected should begin to disappear and be replaced with thoughts of creating a new world around you, filled with loving and caring friends and family.

Allowing yourself to release past frustrations is the beginning of forgiveness. Your willingness to forgive will grow when you can get to a level where the past is just that—the past. To be clear, forgiving anyone is about accepting others where the person is and just allowing them to be. Remember that accepting where they are doesn't necessarily mean being around them.

As I mentioned, I'm now at a place with my former wife where we co-exist. That's to say that whatever happens in her life, as long as there are no adverse effects on our children, is her business. I feel I've recovered so much that I'm genuinely happy for her well-being, without any feelings of regret, anger, or frustration. It has all been accomplished with my willingness to let go of the past, move forward, and internally forgive her. Of course, it would be nice to know if she forgives me, but it really doesn't matter because that's all about her.

Don't Let Fear Hold You Back
"If it is to be, it is up to me."

William H. Johnson

As you're creating your new life, you can start to think about doing some of the things you've thought about doing but might have been afraid to—you know, those things you've always wanted to do but decided not to so you didn't "make waves."

Now that you're starting over, you don't have to ask anyone; nothing in the world should hold you back. Whatever's holding you back is probably one or more of those energy blocks I covered earlier. Release those blocks; they're just your fear.

FEAR is only False Evidence Appearing Real.

The key to moving forward is exposing fears for what they really are—false evidence—and understanding they're keeping you from trying new things, encountering new opportunities, and becoming the new you. You can always revisit the exercises in Step 2: Navigate and ask yourself questions about how real those blocks are.

Practice Gratitude Everyday

A few years ago, my uncle passed away. It's customary in many Jewish communities to not only eulogize the dearly departed at the funeral but also during the first week, about thirty days after, and again at eleven months. This tradition is a way of mourning the person while also celebrating their life.

The subsequent eulogies are called Arayats. At the thirty-day Arayat, one of my uncle's sons spoke. He told a story about when they were going through his father's things and found an interesting letter. It was a letter of thanks to God. It was entitled

"Thank you, Hashem" (the Hebrew version of saying God's name without consecrating His name). My cousin told the audience about the contents of the letter, written over many years, they knew this because it was written in different color inks, and the handwriting was not as clear towards the end of the letter. My uncle read this paper often and added to it over time. For example, when one of his children or grandchildren had an occasion, like a marriage or birth, he would add it to his letter of thanks to Hashem. Everyone at the Arayat was moved by my uncle's continual gesture of gratitude to God.

My cousin went on to tell us a story about his father in the last few months of his life. Those last few years were difficult for my uncle's health, and his movement was limited. He spent most of his time at home. Once, when my cousin visited his parents, he heard his father call out from another room, "Help me!" Startled, my cousin ran to his father's aid, asking what he could do for him. Uncle David calmly looked up at him and said, "Oh, I'm all right. I was speaking to Hashem(God)." My cousin later asked his father about this. My uncle responded with a matter-of-fact answer: "I always talk to Hashem."

This recounting of Uncle David's gratitude to God inspired me to update my own Gratitude Cards. I had written these cards five years earlier while going through my divorce and life coaching school. They cover five areas of my L.I.F.E. - Physical, Financial, Spiritual, Mental, and Emotional. I read them aloud every day. I review and update them frequently to reflect what's current in my life and what I strive to achieve. If you're interested in making your own, I have a brief exercise covering how at the end of this chapter.

A little while after making these gratitude cards, I read a remarkable book called "Becoming Magic" by Genevieve Davis—the same Genevieve Davis I discussed in a previous chapter.[2] In her book, she writes about practicing gratitude twice daily—once in the morning after you wake up and once at night before you sleep. In the book, she also suggests jotting down three things for which you are grateful at that moment.

I decided to take my gratitude cards to another level and purchased a small notebook that fits in my pocket. It wasn't a cheap, flimsy notebook. It was a high-quality journal that looked and felt good, so I would treat the book and the writing exercise with the reverence and respect I wanted to sustain in this daily exercise. Since that day, I have not missed a day of writing in this book twice a day.

Now here's the remarkable culmination of my uncle's Arayats. A few weeks before the eleven-month Arayat, I got a call from my uncle's wife, Aunt Lilli, asking if I would speak at the upcoming event. I told her I would be honored to do so. I hadn't told anyone about my gratitude cards or writings, so I decided to share with my family and friends how inspiring my Uncle David's story was to me. When I finished speaking, the same cousin who spoke at the thirty-day Arayat came over to me and said he was "blown away" by my tribute to his father.

My cousin was the next scheduled speaker, and what he said blew me away! He told the crowd how the letter that inspired me also inspired many others. He gave a few examples, such as how on Yom Kippur, the holiest day in the Jewish year, a day of repentance, and a day of asking for Hashem to give us a good year, the rabbi of his synagogue read Uncle David's letter aloud to his entire congregation. The rabbi used my uncle as an example of the conduct to aim for in life.

Months before the rabbi had done this, my uncle's children, also inspired by the letter, took my uncle's original letter of thanks to Hashem, copied it, and made a binder embossed with the words "Thank You Hashem" in gold on the cover—reproduced in my uncle's handwriting. Then they wrote an introduction in the front of the binder along with the copied original letter. In the introduction, they explained the letter's story and encouraged the holder to continue this act of gratitude on their own.

He then proceeded to open boxes filled with these binders and offered them to anyone in the audience who wanted one to take it, with the proviso that they promised to write in them every day for at least one month. After which time, if they decided not to continue, that would be fine, but he doubted they would ever stop doing it if they kept their promise.

The synchronicity of these events was uncanny. I had no idea my cousins had been working on this. I hadn't told anyone about my gratitude cards or daily writing, and now I understood why my cousin told me he was "blown away." These actions are just one example of how remarkable a simple act of gratitude made by one of the humblest men I ever had the honor of knowing touched so many lives. After the speeches that day, many in the audience approached me and asked if I would share my gratitude cards with them. It filled my heart to think that I could take part in continuing my uncle's legacy in such a beautiful way, so naturally, I did.

Embrace Your Expanded Horizons

It's time to expand your horizons and open your mind to all possibilities. Let's return to the AIM SMART tool you learned in the last chapter. Take this opportunity with your newfound confidence to tackle a goal you may have previously had doubts about being able to reach. Remember to take small steps and set reasonable goals. One of my favorite sayings is, "Inch by inch, it's a cinch; yard by yard, it's hard."

Before I lost 60 pounds, I thought, "I can never lose 60 pounds. It's so much to lose." I was afraid I would fail, so I kept saying, "Why bother? I know I can't do it." Then someone told me about the FEAR acronym. She said I could do it if I broke it down into small portions, like five pounds at a time. I decided I would give it a try.

I only dieted for the first two weeks; I didn't exercise. I rationalized that I had no stamina and couldn't even get through one workout, so why even try? I lost four pounds. This small victory gave me the motivation to start exercising a little bit.

After a week of dieting and light exercise, I lost eight pounds. I was so excited; I couldn't believe it. My enthusiasm grew, and I lost thirty pounds in almost four months because of my new attitude toward eating and exercising. Three months later, I had lost sixty pounds. I took it one step at a time, slowly stretching my comfort zone, and did just a little more each day. The results speak for themselves.

Just like I did, you can break your intimidating goal into small, achievable steps. You can easily make each step along your journey by breaking the goal up over time. Don't beat yourself up if you eat a whole metaphorical pizza one week. Acknowledge that you had the power and made a choice, then adjust your goal and keep moving forward.

Success Activity 12

> Buy a small high-quality journal. Focus on quality so you'll respect and value using it. I recommend Moleskine or something similar.
>
> Every morning and night, write in the journal three things you're grateful for. As time passes, you'll start to see the world differently and appreciate things around you that in the past were commonplace.

Note: You'll notice some Hebrew words written on my cards. I've done my best to translate them for you. I wanted to encourage you to truly be yourself by showing you my cards exactly as they are. Remember to have fun while you're being grateful! :)

TIP 1!

For extra credit, you can print a copy of my gratitude cards and the included blank template in the Activity Book to create your own set of Gratitude Cards.

TIP 2!

I printed 2" x 4" cards (using a sheet of paper 8 1/2 x 11) and laminated them to keep them looking new even after years of use. I made a few sets, which I leave places like my desk and car, so they're an arm's length away whenever the mood strikes.

Read your cards aloud every day. This way, the cards will become ingrained the words will be stored differently than if you read them silently. Repeating them every day will continue to reinforce the words.

Enjoy experiences as they happen! Stay in the moment and appreciate everything around you, no matter the size of the detail.

Chapter 19 — Reclaim

What typically happens in life is that we believe everything anyone and everyone says about us, to the point that we no longer believe in ourselves. You let those detractors we discussed earlier convince us that "I'm not worth it," "I'm not good enough to be happy," and "I don't deserve to feel deeply loved."

I'm here to tell you: That's not true! You deserve to live the happiest life possible. It starts with you taking everything you learned so far and combining it to create the new you and find that unbelievable love you deserve—where you live in the acceptance of "I am a great person, and I'm totally worth it," "I'm awesome and free to be joyful," and "I deserve to feel loved to the max!"

As I've discussed before, the primary purpose of this book is for you to learn how to become the best you possible. As you've seen, the most effective way to do this is to understand who you were before, who you are now, and who you want to be moving forward. You've done fantastic work on who you were and who you are now. It's time to focus on who you want to be. Let's look at the skills you'll need to master to have that life you've always wanted and find that love you've always deserved.

Are You Nice, or Are You Kind?

You've probably heard someone say, "That person is really nice," and thought nothing of it. There's a huge difference between being nice and genuinely kind. To me, nice is holding the door open for others. Kindness, on the other hand, is genuinely caring for a person's well-being—even strangers. Think about it. Have you ever heard of "random acts of niceness"? No, the saying is "random acts of kindness."

In any relationship, practicing kindness will produce fantastic results. If you're truly kind, the results will be more about the great inner feeling it gives you than what you'll get in return. I'm not saying you shouldn't get kindness back, but don't set an expectation for it, and you'll never be disappointed. If you have kids, you probably understand the concept of unconditional love. You love your kids unconditionally, meaning there are no strings attached. You don't expect anything in return, not even a thank you.

The best thing you can do as you develop new relationships is to build them based on kindness, with absolutely no strings attached. Call it "unconditional kindness." As the connection grows, the kindness will increase, and if there is true respect between the two of you, it will develop into a natural, healthy relationship. I like to practice unconditional kindness with everyone I meet; even if I never see that person again, I know that I made their day a little better, and who doesn't need more of that?

This same approach can be used to repair existing relationships that have become distant or strained. Unconditional kindness can break through relationship barriers and get everyone ready to engage in the relationship again, even if the relationship needs to evolve—as it did for my ex-wife and me.

You may encounter skepticism when you first begin using unconditional kindness. This can be especially true if you pair it with other tools you've learned in this book, such as Stop, Think, and Respond. You may surprise everyone in your life as you step into being the new you. This response is normal. They are still used to you 1.0 and will take some time to get used to you 2.0.

The key during your transformation is to keep your focus fixed on the goals you created in the Visualize step. As you continue to move forward toward your long-term goal, over time, everyone around you will begin to understand that the new you is here to stay.

The Abundant W.A.R.R.I.OR. Mindset:
The 7 Secrets to An Abundant Mindset

It can be challenging to remember to have an abundant mindset during stressful events, so before we close out the UNCOVER process, I want to leave you with one more acronym—WARRIOR—as a quick reference during challenging times. Remember: situations and circumstances will always go sideways, but you have the power to adjust your mindset and find the abundance in every situation.

W: Wisdom

Seeking wisdom and continuing your journey of learning are essential steps in developing and maintaining an abundant mindset. Albert Einstein said, "Wisdom is not a product of schooling but of the lifelong attempt to acquire it." We always want to be in a state of receiving, especially when learning. The more open you are to learning, changing, and growing, the more your abundant mindset will grow! Wisdom comes from examining your experiences and the things you've learned to understand how best to respond to situations with grace and compassion (abundance) rather than with fear and anxiety (lack).

A: Ask, Act & Attitude

We discussed this earlier in the book: "The Cycle of "A's." Ask for what you want to happen in your life, act responsibly to help it happen, and have a great attitude while you work toward making it happen. The key during this process is to relax and sink into the process.

Focusing intently on what you don't yet have can actually push it further away. Accepting the journey as you act can help bring your goals closer. Meditation, deep breathing, journaling, and exercise can help you calm your nervous system and focus your attention on the abundance already around you as you manifest even more abundance in your life!

>   Ask: Let the universe know what you want.
>   Act: Take the steps you need to reach your goal.
>   Attitude: Keep a positive attitude to keep moving toward your goal!

R: Realize

Realize stands for being content and having an attitude that reflects "I have everything!" When developing an abundant mindset, it's important to stay calm and not get upset about how things turn out. Thinking about how much you want something steals energy away from other parts of your life and takes control of your thinking. This can radically change how you interact with the world because your focus will be on getting whatever you want, while everything else in your life suffers because you're spending all your mental energy wanting. Focus instead on everything you DO have in your life! This will attract more to you.

R: Recognize

Recognize when to express thanks in your life. Feeling and expressing gratitude is incredibly important! Practice gratitude for everything in your life, big and small. A helpful activity to kick-start gratitude is writing down three things you're grateful for in the morning and three things at night. Another easy way to start is by saying thank you to everyone for everything. The more you say thank you, the more you will feel it. Express gratitude to your friends, family, and even strangers. When you are genuine and show gratitude and appreciation, the people in your life will also begin expressing appreciation to you! Genuine gratitude is one of the quickest ways to have an abundant mindset!

I: Imagine

"Shoot for the moon. Even if you miss, you'll be among the stars."

Norman Vincent Peale,
The Power of Positive Thinking

A huge part of abundance is imagination! The more you allow your imagination to thrive, the more abundance you'll have. Your imagination is your inner self telling you what you want. Let your imagination express your soul's desires! Sometimes it's easy to imagine things but difficult to see them manifesting in the physical world. To help keep your momentum, celebrate when you achieve every step toward your goals. Additionally, tell someone you trust about your dreams to stay accountable in manifesting them!

O: Optimistic

Optimistic means finding the positive in everything. Be positive about everything in your life, and refrain from complaining. When you complain, you're letting negative thinking creep into your mind, and you begin to approach life from a position of lack rather than abundance. This can lead to experiencing negative thoughts about how nothing is going right in your life or how nothing is going your way. It can also lead to blaming others for what seems to be going sideways in your life. The truth is your happiness is all inside you. The more you think happy thoughts, the more happy, positive things will be drawn to you and into your life.

Note: This does NOT mean ignoring things that need fixing. I'm not advocating for toxic positivity. I'm advocating for a fundamental mindset shift.

R: Resilient

Being resilient means being flexible and having an open mind. What you want may not manifest immediately or in ways you initially anticipated. Hurdles might crop up, but don't these discourage you! Be ready to be flexible and adjust on the fly. Don't get upset when things don't go as you were hoping. If you did everything you could to accomplish your goals and they still didn't turn out the way you hoped, it probably means it wasn't supposed to happen for you that way. Look at what happened and be flexible. Being flexible means being ready to change. When you're ready to change, you are willing to grow in the ways you need to ensure the things you want can happen the way they need to for the best outcome.

Chapter 20 — Financial Abundance

I have one more tool for you to put in your transformation toolbox. This last action chapter addressed one of the top causes of relationship arguments: finances. The mindset of financial abundance is one of the more difficult mindsets to achieve for most people. That's understandable. No matter what your financial status is at this moment, I'm sure there's at least a bit of financial insecurity.

As humans, we don't like insecurity in any area of our lives, but this is particularly true of the resource we use to procure basic needs. There is a reason Maslow built an entire theory based on the changes that can be seen in human behavior as the stability of needs satisfaction is disrupted.

You may be experiencing this yourself. Even after all the work you've done, you may still catch yourself thinking things like: Do I have enough saved to cover my bills or any unexpected expenses? How am I going to make my next payments? What will my financial future look like? I can't afford to go on vacation, buy a car, have fun, or donate to charity.

All these worries can lead you back to the mindset of lack you have been addressing. The tricky aspect is that the more this mindset is in place, the more it perpetuates and builds on itself. Remember that even when these thoughts creep in—regardless of your income level and financial circumstances—you can always change your mindset by taking actionable steps.

I'll be frank, it will probably be a bit difficult in the beginning, even with all the work you've been doing on mindset. You will likely question yourself and the value and validity of this process. Finances hit some visceral part inside the way that other issues don't. When these feelings come up, don't be surprised, and don't say I didn't warn you.

Big Four Accounts Breakdown

How can you make these changes? Let's get into details of the system that helped me radically shift my mindset around finances.

You can use cash or open separate bank accounts for this approach. There are banks these days that allow you to set up sub-accounts from your bank account for just such accounts. I like the feeling of the cash in my hands and counting it whenever the need or desire arises. Something about the feel of the cash in my hands gives me a rush. I'm also very visual, so seeing the physical currency helps me track how much I have.

To start, take a percentage, ideally 40%, of your income and any other money that comes your way. Put all of it aside. If 40% is too much for you, start with a lower number and work up to 40%.

We're going to take this 40% and put them into four accounts:
- Big Purchases
- Fun Money
- Giving to Others (Charity)
- Golden Goose/ Emergency/Pay Down Debts (like credit cards or loans)

You'll be putting 10% into each of these accounts. I use a spreadsheet like Google Sheets to track my progress. A date column and a notes column are included in my spreadsheet to make it easy to review my financial activity. When I deposit my 10% into each account, I enter them into my Google Sheets spreadsheet. I also enter those changes each time I spend money from any of the accounts. I like to use Google Spreadsheets because it's always accessible, even when I'm away from my laptop. I downloaded the app to my smartphone to use it there as well.

When I decided to implement this financial abundance plan, I was not in a good place financially, and the thought of taking any percentage out of my income was ludicrous. But I decided to trust the process. I wanted to achieve a mindset of abundance in all aspects of my life. And even though it made me uncomfortable, I realized that staying in my comfort zone would not shift my mindset of lack around money unless I made some hard choices. The payoff has been fantastic. It helped me financially and in all other areas of my life.

Big Purchases Account

This account is for those unexpected bills that pop up when you aren't expecting them to: your car breaks down, you need to buy a new appliance, or you have an unexpected medical expense. You can also use it to save for something you want in the future: a big gift, a new car, or a house—whatever you need it for.

When you have money set aside for surprise expenses, you automatically reduce the worry and stress that can occur in these situations. Doing this will also allow you to focus more energy on addressing the situation without wearing yourself thin.

I'll give you an example. I took my car in for what I thought was a simple oil change and tune-up, maybe a $100 expense. About an hour later, I got a call from the dealership telling me I needed new brakes, tire rotation, and a few other things to the tune of $500. Instead of panicking and wondering, "How am I going to pay this from my everyday bills?" I took out my big purchase account and saw I had more than I needed in the account. This account helped me pay the mechanic's bill without missing a beat. Knowing that I already had money set aside in my big purchase account felt so good.

Fun Money Account

We're often so busy doing life we forget to enjoy and live LIFE! Doing life is just trudging along and going through the motions.

Have you ever seen the movie Joe Versus the Volcano? It's an obscure, campy movie starring Tom Hanks and Meg Ryan. Tom Hanks plays an average Joe, going to work every day, sitting at his desk watching the fluorescent light fixture above him flicker. Joe's face, entire demeanor, body, and wardrobe are pale and sickly looking. The only object with any color in his life is a tropical beach lamp he keeps on his desk, symbolizing the life he wants, but believes he'll never attain. He was endlessly going through the motions, resigned to a miserable existence. I bring this up to let you know you don't have to follow his example!

That's where the Fun Money Account comes in, so you can indulge by doing something fun NOW rather than waiting for some far-off goal to be achieved. It could be anything you consider fun: going to a concert, an expensive dinner, or shopping for clothes you might not normally buy. Maybe you'd like to do some fun activities: going to a sporting event, or maybe you're adventurous and want to go skydiving! Whatever it is, this account is for you to have fun with.

The idea behind the Fun Money Account is that many of us want to do fun things, but we usually allow our mindset of lack to dominate our thought process. The "lack" mindset can be infectious; it could start by thinking about one area in your life where you say you can't afford something. Then, the next thing you know, it infects other areas of your life, and you start pinching pennies and obsessing over every dollar you spend. It becomes like a pressure gauge as you begin stewing over the things you can't have until you eventually get to the point you explode on someone who tells you a bill has to be paid immediately. Your spouse, kids, or some innocent bystander who happens to be the messenger of the bad news bill may be left in the wreckage after you over-pressurize.

The point is that by setting up these accounts—especially the Fun Money Account—you're allowing yourself to change your mindset of lack and "I can't afford it" to a mindset of abundance and "How can I afford it?" Sometimes, you may look at your Fun

Account and say, "Hey! I have the money to buy the thing!" Other times, you may discover, "Ok, I have this much; the thing costs that much, so by this date in the future, I can do it!"

I've used my Fun Money for vacations and a new TV, and I even bought an expensive pair of sunglasses. Recently while we were on vacation, my sunglasses broke. I had never paid more than $50 for sunglasses before, but while we were walking around, I decided to indulge and buy $250 sunglasses. For me, that's extravagant; it's like going to a ridiculously overpriced restaurant and spending over $100 for a steak! I typically don't do it. But I wanted new sunglasses, and my fun account had the money, so I went crazy and got them. I even explained to the salespeople what I was doing. They loved it and asked me to explain the four-account system to them.

Think about the effects using this approach will have on your psyche! Handling your finances is where the rubber meets the road; you will see your abundance mindset growing in real-time. If, like me, you're visual, it's much easier to watch your mindset shift when handling physical assets. You're flexing your new abundance muscle! And you're feeling good about yourself and your decisions that led to your ability to indulge like this! Feels great, doesn't it?

Giving to Others Account

As I've mentioned before, I'm Jewish—Modern Orthodox—and as an expression of that, I observe the laws of the Torah. One of those laws is called Tithing or Maaser. It's taking a percentage of your income and giving it to charity—Tzedakah in Hebrew. The traditionally accepted amount is 10%, so that's what we'll use here.

While charity is a commandment, there's something rewarding about making donations. Often, people say, "I'd like to give charity, but I need charity myself." This thought pattern is a deep level of a "lack" mindset!

Assigning the Giving Account a name makes it more important and intimate for you. You might want to label this account for a specific group or someone in your life you want to help: the American Cancer Fund, the ALS Foundation, the local food fund, or Grandma's daily expenses account. It's up to you. Another thing, it's a good idea to let this account grow to at least $100 or $200 before using it. The impact will be greater for the recipient and for you, the giver.

On a side note, there's a concept in Judaism that when you donate from your heart, God will give it back to you tenfold. Of course, there's no hard evidence to prove it. But I've heard countless stories of people who give, and without any reason, they find themselves with a lot more money in short order.

A good friend of mine, Jack Doueck, wrote a book called "The Chesed Boomerang."[1] Roughly translated from Hebrew, chesed means kindness. The word has a much deeper and more nuanced meaning, but we'll use "kindness" as the meaning for this purpose. The premise of his book is that when you give kindness—any kindness: money, time, food, anything—it comes back to you like a boomerang and is more incredible than when you performed the act of kindness.

For our purposes here of Financial Abundance: By allocating that percentage for charity or others in need, you can foster that mindset of abundance by being able to help others. When the opportunity arises, by living in your mindset of abundance, you can go into this account and use the funds for giving without feeling like it hurts or takes away from your life. You'll feel free and comfortable when giving rather than grudging and forced.

Recently, my brother-in-law had a cancer scare. Thank God he went into remission and beat it after chemos and surgeries. The whole family was so happy because his original prognosis was not good. We were all concerned about his health. Soon after his diagnosis, my sister emailed me that she and my brother-in-law were participating in a 5K run and looking for donations. My heart leaped at the opportunity to donate, especially since my charity fund had more than enough to make a decent contribution.

I could give fully from the heart and with a beautiful feeling. You'll have the opportunity to feel the same way when you give back.

Golden Goose/Emergency/Pay Down Debts Account

Let your imagination run wild here. This account could be for whatever you want and allows you to save in another area. It can be for emergencies, paying down debt, future planning, or a golden goose account to build your retirement nest egg. The point is that this account allows you to save for whatever! Reduce debt, invest in your future, or help someone struggling who might not be covered in your charity account.

As I said, these four accounts aim to help the most difficult area of your mindset transformation, shifting from lack to abundance, by being diligent with every penny. Whenever anything comes up, you'll get to the point that you won't have to think twice about it. Either you'll have the money already allocated, or you'll be able to plan for the expense without the stress normally associated with money decisions.

Success Activity 13a

> Create a worksheet using Google Sheets or an Excel spreadsheet. Use the four accounts you create to make four columns across the top of the spreadsheet.

Success Activity 13b

> When you receive any money—salary, investment dividends, profits from business adventures, even cash gifts—take 40% (or whatever amount you decided), split it into four equal parts, and put the money into each account. If the accounts are online, transfer the funds into the appropriate accounts; if you decide to use cash, put the appropriate amount in each envelope.

Note: If you're not tech-savvy or prefer pen and paper, you can print the ledger out and handwrite your entries.

TIP!

Recording both deposits and withdrawals is important so you also acknowledge purchases and charities. You're recognizing what's going out and coming in, taking greater responsibility for everything going on in your L.I.F.E.

As you move forward using this method, the best advice I can give you is: Be diligent and don't second-guess yourself!

Chapter 21 — Closing Thoughts

Congratulations. I'm so proud of you for completing this book. You should be proud of yourself. It's a significant accomplishment. Give yourself the credit you deserve. According to a study published in the Journal of Clinical Psychology, people who set a clear goal were over ten times more likely to be "continuously successful" in their goal six months later.[1] If you've been completing the activities in the workbook, you've likely made progress toward the goals you set in Chapter 17. Celebrate your accomplishments!

As your outlook on your L.I.F.E. starts to change from lack to abundance, from self-conscious to self-aware, you'll notice things differently. Some things you may experience are:

- You will express gratitude and appreciation instead of complaining and blaming.
- You will have more conversations than confrontations,
- Your stress level will start to reduce.
- You will be thriving instead of striving.
- You look forward to seeing friends, family, and colleagues instead of dreading it.

- As situations arise, you will be looking for opportunities instead of problems.

Your journey from Worrier to Warrior is always progressing. You now have the tools to radically change your life so you can Live Incredibly Full Everyday. Tools like: The Cycle of A's, Stop, Think and Respond, AIM SMART, and Financial Abundance.

The beauty of this book is that you can always reread any or all of it whenever you need a refresher.

Let's look at some examples. Imagine you find yourself in a situation where your usual action used to be to REACT. To shoot first and ask questions later. Now you understand why that approach doesn't work. I like to say, "If you shoot first, you can't really ask questions later because everyone is dead!"—at least emotionally. So instead of being an emotional sniper, you can now start using Stop, Think and Respond!

Remember, scoring a "10" on the Success Activity scorecard will take time. But along the way, you're building your emotional muscle memory every time you implement even small parts of the exercise. And as we discussed, if explosions do happen as you begin using these tools, you can always go back to the person, ask for forgiveness, and build on that.

How about The Cycle of A's? Have you put it into motion? Have you Asked, Acted, and had the right Attitude? How were your results?

If you have, it probably didn't go exactly as you hoped the first time. Or it did, and you considered it a coincidence. Remember, it wasn't. It's the Magic starting to happen; build on it and stay with the Attitude of not getting emotionally tied to the outcome.

Have you started the four accounts for your Financial Abundance? Remember, you don't have to start at 40%. Come up with a number you're comfortable with for now, and as you start to see and feel the difference, you can increase the amount you put aside into your four accounts. Just start with SOMETHING.

CHAPTER 21—CLOSING THOUGHTS • 171

Let's be honest. We both know it's true, so let's address the elephant in the room. Sometimes things aren't going well, and you will slip into the mindset of lack, self-consciousness, and questioning yourself. As I've written before, I sometimes fall into those moments, too. Don't worry; that's normal and to be expected.

Remember, we're not looking for perfection. Perfection doesn't exist. It's about progress. There will be days that are not so great, so don't get down on yourself; chalk it up to a slip and, as soon as you can, find a way to shift your mindset. There are easy ways to do that. Come back to the book when you need to, find a passage that resonated with you, and review it to center yourself again.

You can also get my Worrier To Warrior Card Deck if you need a portable reminder to carry in your pocket or bag. I designed these cards to be an easy way to carry around the main principle of my course, so you don't have to carry around this book to have the tools at hand. The card deck is for you to use when you're doubting yourself. You can make it a daily habit of pulling out a card from the deck, reading the principle, and thinking about how it can help you today.

I wrote this book based on my experiences and that of others, like my clients. The systems and techniques you have learned were developed and cultivated over fifteen years of trial and error. I'm telling you this because I want you to know that anything worth having—like a happy, full L.I.F.E., takes work and sacrifice.

The personal sacrifices I made along the way were to recognize and step away from the tendencies holding me back. It was that simple. Yet it was not easy. It took work and a desire to keep moving forward in the process. Giving up was something I was very good at in my Martin 1.0 life. I cannot count how often I gave up on myself or the people and things around me. Rather than work through situations, I would default to being a people pleaser, a control freak, or needing recognition, acknowledgment, and validation. In my mind, I rationalized (Rational-lied) that "I had no choice; I had to DO something!" when this was really all to feed my ego. Worst of all, I had a short temper, and everyone around me would pay the price for my shortcomings.

Through my willingness to change and become a better version of myself, I learned that I almost always have a choice (again, I don't believe in absolutes).

Recently in a podcast interview, I was asked about the phrase "I can't" and how paralyzing the statement was. This phrase has the power to hold someone back from what they really want because of two simple words—"I can't." As we discussed the concept on the podcast, I realized the "I can't" phrase was something I used to use daily. Now, as a result of all the work I did on myself and constantly continue to do, the amount of time I even think the phrase is next to never (again, no absolutes).

I've referenced people like Genevieve Davis, who have coached and mentored me through my journey. The help of those mentors has helped me become who I am today and who I continue to evolve into becoming. The support and guidance from others are now a constant in my L.I.F.E. The people who coach and mentor me may not be constant; the coaches and mentors change as I change and as my needs change. Having support is now a non-negotiable for me, and it should be a non-negotiable for you too.

I heard this saying over ten years ago, "Even the best coaches have coaches." Recently I heard someone say, "Every entrepreneur needs a coach." I may be the coach you're looking for. I may not be, but that's okay. It's not about me; it's about you. Find someone who can fill that role for you. It may be multiple people for different parts of your L.I.F.E.—one for your personal life, one for your professional life, and another for a specific task or project you need guidance with. My point is: don't go it alone; you don't have to.

It could be you want me to be your coach or one of your coaches. We can have a conversation and see if we're a good fit. If we are a fit, great! If not, that's okay! Find someone who is.

At one point, when I was at a low financial point, I rationalized (there's the Rational Lied again) I couldn't afford to have a coach. Nothing could have been further from the truth! The truth is I couldn't afford NOT to have a coach. A good coach is an investment, not an expense or a cost. It's normal to need help letting things go, making goals, or sticking with your plan. Don't deny yourself growth due to fear.

Remember, this is a continuing journey. You're always learning and growing. It's okay if you stumble. It's going to happen. I'm looking for you to make slow, steady, sustainable changes for the long haul. It's how you respond to these situations instead of react. That one step will begin to make a difference.

My hope for you is that you take this book and apply everything you learned in your L.I.F.E. Start every morning with gratitude. Pull out the pocket journal you got in Chapter 18 and write three things you're grateful for. Next, take a moment and be spiritual. Whatever that means to you. For me, it means praying every day. For you, it could be praying, meditating, or simply acknowledging your higher power. Holding on to faith is more important than you think. You're giving yourself room to recognize that everything that happens is not always in your power. That higher power is there to help you get what you want; accept it. You can think about The Cycle of A's if that helps. Say your mantra aloud, whatever it may be. For me, It's "I Live Incredibly Full Everyday." I know that for NFL quarterback great Tom Brady, it's reciting The 4 Agreements by Don Miguel Ruiz. The idea here is to find something that works for you. This practice starts your day with an attitude of looking for opportunities instead of problems. Smile at everyone you see, friends, family, colleagues, and strangers. Especially strangers!

You might want to adopt my "laugh quota." Every day I go out and make someone laugh—preferably a stranger. Then I thank them for letting me fill my quota of making someone laugh at least once a day. This personalizes the quota for the other person and lets them know my intention to spread laughter, happiness, and joy. After making that connection, I ask them to pass it along. So why not take this daily quota up yourself?

Maybe we can start a movement to spread happiness, understanding, and acceptance of others with the simple act of sharing laughter and passing it on. Be a Changemaker. You can even say you are Paying It Forward. Does it matter if you know the other person? Of course not! It's about adding a bit of sunshine to someone else's L.I.F.E.! Not only will you make that person feel good, but you will also feel great.

If you get nothing else out of this book, I hope you get this: How you approach every day is only up to you, no one else. No matter what's going on in your L.I.F.E. it's up to you.

Go out and Enjoy L.I.F.E. so you can
Live Incredibly Full Everyday!

Scan Me!

Next Steps

You may be thinking "What's my next step?" "How do I keep this momentum going?"

Momentum is a product of Inspiration. Inspiration comes from something deep inside of you telling you to do something.

Are you feeling inspired by what you read and do you want to continue your journey to Enjoy L.I.F.E. so you can Live Incredibly Full Everyday?

Are you ready to take action and do something? If your answer is yes, visit the link or scan the QR Code on the previous page for a special gift from me. Let's create the world you want together.

Until we meet again,
Have a great day, remember to Enjoy L.I.F.E. and...

Live Incredibly Full Everyday!

Martin

References

Chapter 2 — Origins of The Warrior's L.I.F.E. Code
1. Salama, Martin. *Recovering From Divorce*. 1st ed. Lulu.com, 2013.

Chapter 4 — The Cycle of A's (Ask, Act, Attitude)
1. Davis, Genevieve. *Becoming Magic: A Course in Manifesting an Exceptional Life* (Book 1). Createspace, 2014.
2. Losier, Michael J. *Law of Attraction: The science of attracting more of what you want and less of what you don't*. New York, NY: Grand Central Publishing, 2019.
3. Aaron Doughty. *How The Law Of Attraction REALLY WORKS! (Manifest Anything You Want) | John Assaraf. Youtube.com.*, 2022. https://www.youtube.com/watch?v=yDgGp5HZhrw.

Chapter 6 — Think
1. Ruiz, Miguel. *The Four Agreements: A Practical Guide to Personal Freedom*. San Rafael, CA: Amber-Allen Pub., 1997.
2. Salama, Martin. *Recovering From Divorce*. 1st ed. Lulu.com, 2013.
3. Davis, Genevieve. *Becoming Magic: A Course in Manifesting an Exceptional Life* (Book 1). Createspace, 2014.

Chapter 8 — Putting It All Together

1. Pausch, Randy, Jeffrey Zaslow, and Jai Pausch. *The Last Lecture.* New York, NY: Hachette Books, 2018.
2. Lerner, Harriet Goldhor. *Why won't you apologize?: Healing big betrayals and everyday hurts.* New York, NY: Touchstone, 2017.
3. Brown, Brené. *"I'm Sorry: How to Apologize and Why It Matters." Episode.* Unlocking Us, May 6, 2020. https://brenebrown.com/podcast/harriet-lerner-and-brene-im-sorry-how-to-apologize-why-it-matters-part-1-of-2/

Chapter 13 — Navigate

1. Wrench, John S., Narissra M. Punyanunt-Carter, and Katherine S. Thweatt. "Chapter 9: Conflict in Relationships." In *Interpersonal Communication: A Mindful Approach to Relationships.* San Francisco, CA: Open SUNY, 2020.

Chapter 17 — Visualize

1. Wissman, Barret. "An Accountability Partner Makes You Vastly More Likely to Succeed." *Entrepreneur.com*, March 20, 2018. https://www.entrepreneur.com/leadership/an-accountability-partner-makes-you-vastly-more-likely-to/310062.

Chapter 18 — Embrace & Enjoy

1. Salama, Martin. Recovering From Divorce. 1st ed. Lulu.com, 2013.
2. Davis, Genevieve. *Becoming Magic: A Course in Manifesting an Exceptional Life* (Book 1). Createspace, 2014.

Chapter 20 — Financial Abundance

1. Doueck, Jack. *The chesed boomerang: How acts of kindness enrich our lives.* Deal, NJ: Yagdiyl Torah, 1999.

Chapter 21 — Closing Thoughts

1. Norcross, John C., Marci S. Mrykalo, and Matthew D. Blagys. "*Auld Lang Syne: Success Predictors, Change Processes, and Self-Reported Outcomes of New Year's Resolvers and Nonresolvers.*" Journal of Clinical Psychology 58, no. 4 (April 2002): 397–405. https://doi.org/10.1002/jclp.1151.

Scan Me!

To visit ConnectwithMartin.com
to access more tools and resources, or
to book Martin as a speaker.

Want to be able to carry these tools everywhere with you, but don't want to lug around a book?

Scan the QR code to grab a deck of the Worrier to Warrior cards!

The Author

Martin Salama has four children and eight grandchildren from his first marriage. In June 2018, Martin married Sarita. They live with Sarita's three children in Brooklyn, New York.

Besides his family, one of Martin's proudest personal accomplishments is being a founder, and the original president of the first synagogue in Eatontown called Shaare Tefilah Bene Moshe, named in memory of his brother Michael. The synagogue currently has a congregation consisting of over four hundred families.

When Martin isn't coaching, or speaking on podcasts and stages, he loves to cook. One of his greatest joys is watching his family and friends gather and enjoy each other's company while savoring his meals.

www.ingramcontent.com/pod-product-compliance
Lightning Source LLC
Chambersburg PA
CBHW050905160426
43194CB00011B/2300